Grace
for the Journey

A Widow's Walk Through the
Psalms with God

From Grief to Healing

30 Day Devotional and Journal

Sherry Brooks-Medley

Grace for the Journey
A Widow's Walk through the Psalms with God
From Grief to Healing
30 Day Devotional and Journal

Published by
Kingdom Publishing, LLC
Odenton, Maryland U.S.A.

Printed in the U.S.A.

Copyright ©2022 by Sherry Brooks-Medley

All rights reserved. No part of this book may be reproduced, stored in retrieval system, or transmitted in any form or by any means—electronic, mechanical, photocopy, recording, or otherwise—except as may be expressly permitted by the 1976 Copyright Act or for brief quotations in printed reviews, without the prior written permission of the author.

Unless otherwise indicated, all Scripture quotations are taken from the Holy Bible, King James Version (Public Domain). Scripture quotations marked NKJV are taken from the New King James Version®, copyright ©1982 by Thomas Nelson, Inc. Used by permission. All rights reserved. Scriptures marked CEV are taken from the CONTEMPORARY ENGLISH VERSION (CEV): Scripture taken from the CONTEMPORARY ENGLISH VERSION copyright ©1995 by the American Bible Society. Used by permission. Scriptures marked NIV are taken from the NEW INTERNATIONAL VERSION (NIV): Scripture taken from THE HOLY BIBLE, NEW INTERNATIONAL VERSION®. Copyright ©1973, 1978, 1984, 2011 by Biblica, Inc.™. Used by permission. Scriptures marked NAS are taken from the NEW AMERICAN STANDARD (NAS): Scripture taken from the NEW AMERICAN STANDARD BIBLE®, copyright© 1960, 1962, 1963, 1968, 1971, 1972, 1973, 1975, 1977, 1985 by The Lockman Foundation. Used by permission. Scriptures marked NLT are taken from the HOLY BIBLE, NEW LIVING TRANSLATION (NLT): Scriptures taken from the HOLY BIBLE, NEW LIVING TRANSLATION, copyright© 1996, 2004, 2007 by Tyndale House Foundation. Used by permission of Tyndale House Publishers, Inc., Carol Stream, Illinois 60188. All rights reserved. Used by permission.

Paperback ISBN: 978-1-947741-66-9
E-book ISBN: 978-1-947741-67-6

Disclaimer Statement:

The pages of this book are the reflections, thoughts, spiritual experiences and beliefs of the author. The statements in this book have not been evaluated by professional grief counselors. Please be advised to seek medical/professional counseling and guidance during your time of grief. This book is not intended to diagnose, to treat or to substitute for grief counseling.

"When you left, so did a part of my soul."
~Sherry Medley~

This book is dedicated to my devoted and loving husband
who left us too soon.
Raymond Edward Medley, Sr.
and his legacy

"A Part of My Soul Feels So Lost Without You" ~ Your Wife

If you simply cannot understand why someone is
grieving so much for so long,
then consider yourself FORTUNATE
that you do not understand.

~Joanne Cacciatore~

Acknowledgements

God, thank you for giving me Grace for the Journey.

There is no way I could have made it through the grief process without a community and village of family and friends who love my children and me. I wish to acknowledge those who stood by me in prayer, support and love. I extend my heartfelt gratitude to my loving and devoted mom, Rosemary Brooks who is my rock, and my sisters, Betty Brooks (who stayed up and listened to my late-night readings), and Joyce Brooks (my Aaron, always holding me up in my time of need).

In remembrance of my sisters Gloria Ann Brooks and Marguerite (LuLu) Underdue; thank you, LuLu for the times you encouraged me and said, "There is always somebody that needs to hear what you have to say; just write your story." I hope you can hear me from my heart to heaven.

My besties, Valerie Lawrence, Lisha Jones, Cheryl Williams, Cecelia Smith and Willie Pinkney, who never left my side. Helen Brown and Marsella Hare for their support and prayer covering. The spiritual leadership of my Pastor and friend, Apostle, Dr. Craig Coates, Pastor, Dr. Karen Johnson (my Mentor), and Pastor Raleigh Medley (my awesome Brother-in-Law), who is my husband's best friend.

Most of all, I have been forever blessed with my phenomenal children, who were my greatest supporters, Raymond Medley Jr, John Medley, Joy Medley, and Joshua Medley. They took on the mantle, fortitude, and the continued love of their father to strengthen me for this journey during my most difficult days. I extend my sincere appreciation to the vast amount of people who provided love and support. I truly thank you from the very depths of my heart.

I extend my sincere appreciation to the vast amount of people who provided love and support. I truly thank each of you from the very depths of my heart.

Apostle Antonio Palmer of Kingdom Publishing, thank you for your support and patience in helping me bring my vision and dream to pass.

Grief is learning to live with
someone in your heart
instead of your arms.

~Lynda Cheldelin Fell~

Foreword from the Children

The origins of this book lie in a widow's tears. They are tears we wish were never shed, tears that drowned us in sorrow and despair, and tears that left us gasping for air.

However, over time, these widow's tears became a reflection of the Balm of Gilead. Each teardrop would leave an imprint so visible and firmly etched that its transformative effect could not be denied. No longer did these tears bring sorrow or despair but were exchanged for strength and healing.

Healing cascades out of this book like a flood and prayerfully will become the balm you have been seeking. As we watched our Mother go through the lowest of lows of losing someone she loved, we witnessed her walking through the weakest moment in her life and turning it into her greatest strength.

All of us know that death is the final outcome of life. However, it has been said, "No one is actually dead until the ripples they cause in the world die away." Our Father was a jolly man who was always willing to lend a helping hand, no matter the situation. And it seems, even in death, he is carrying on this legacy.

Your Beloved Children,
Raymond Medley Jr, John Medley
Joy Medley, Joshua Medley

Foreword

A sign of a true and authentic author is the writer's knowledge of the subject detailed in the pages of their story. In order for a person to share their story, there must be evidence of an experience that changed their perspective and even the direction of their path. The validation of that author is the reader. Yes, the reader must identify with the characters and the experience. Although it may not have been their experience, the reader is given the opportunity to "ride-along" for the journey.

One of my favorite cartoons from back-in-the-day was Dora the Explorer. What I loved so much was the manner in which she and her friends journeyed to discover new things. One of the regular characters, The Map, would be sought out for his unique gifting. "I'm the map," he would exclaim. And then the journey would begin. In short, Dora and her friends embarked upon a voyage that would be full of unexpected discoveries and experiences. During this process, child viewers would be exposed to a new language while experiencing life through Dora's eyes.

As uncanny as it might seem, Dora's story mirrors our lives. We are on a journey that leads to new and unexpected discoveries about ourselves and the world around us. Although we experience joy, unlike Dora, we inadvertently must experience pain. Sometimes the pain doesn't make sense; that is until time reveals the reason for the suffering. The Apostle Paul defines suffering as evidence that agape love is present. He actually terms it as longsuffering. The Greek word markrothymeos is defined as being of long spirit, not to lose heart. It is to persevere patiently and bravely in enduring misfortunes. This is a quality that one can only experience in relationships! True love must have longsuffering as one of its main attributes.

God the Father demonstrated this level of love for humanity when He sent Jesus to die for us. Jesus immediately accepted the task. He took off His kingship and entered the world, pre-positioned for a journey of suffering and pain. Who knew that part of demonstrating this love for us would require Him to be tried, scourged, beaten, and crucified?

I propose such a journey was even hidden from Jesus, that He might fully redeem mankind. Furthermore, He would set forth the example of husband and wife, as stated in Ephesians 5. Yet, at the end of his earthly journey, even Jesus asked the Father if it were possible to remove the pain and suffering He would endure. His resolve was to accept the will of God.

All of this makes theological sense, but is it possible to endure pain and suffering in our present day? Is there joy in suffering? Let me just say that the author clearly defines joy, pain, suffering, and purpose in the book. Pain, in this case, fully defines her God-intended purpose. My mind reverts to the first in a chain of traumatic events, circumventing the author's life story. We were attending the funeral of her sister, Gloria. I remember the day as if it were yesterday.

A mutual friend of ours, Bishop Sterling Porter and I were having a conversation about an observation; Sherry's circle of influence was like that of a Pastor. Both Sterling and I knew those words would not be a welcomed conversation with Sherry! She never wanted the spotlight and was happy with just serving. In our observation, it was clear that God's hand was on her for a greater purpose and more pronounced than working in the background. We both agreed, she is the one and her time was at hand. Likewise, we both decided this was not the time to have that conversation with Sherry.

The very next day after Sherry buried her sister Gloria, she and I were having a conversation in the midst of conducting business. She was preparing for an event that attracts consumers from every part of our county when I asked the question, "When will you take the time to grieve your loss?" Her response was, "Not right now; I don't have the time." Little did either of us know that in the process of a few hours, tragedy would strike again, leaving us all traumatized.

The moment I received the call from the police officer on the scene, I stood in a daze telling myself this could not be. God certainly would not allow this to happen right after we just buried Gloria. The officer informed me that he needed to reach Sherry. I thought to myself, "How in the world will she handle this?" At that moment, I was convinced that God really does put more on you than you can bear, and Sherry was about to experience this first-hand!

One week later, I spoke these words to a broken, shattered and devastated woman, "Sherry, this makes no sense right now, but you will get better, just not now." Months later, God gave me the grace to share with her that this pain was for a greater purpose, one she would not readily embrace except by the grace of God.

As you read this book, keep in mind that although it is Sherry's journey, God is the true author of her story. He chose her to walk it out, and what an amazing journey! I am confident that you will identify with Sherry's pain and appreciate the grace that is yet upon her life and her journey.

Apostle Craig Coates, Ph.D.
Founder, Fresh Start Church and
Triumphant Church Assemblies

If I had my life to live again,
next time I would find you sooner
so I could love you longer.
~Unknown~

Table of Content

Reality: Losing our Superman	page	1
The Day I Will Never Forget	page	5
God's Call for the Journey	page	10
Day 1 She is Courageous	page	13
Day 2 God is Our Safe Place	page	19
Day 3 God's Guiding Light	page	23
Day 4 From Trauma to Trust to Triumph	page	27
Day 5 Grief is on a One-Way Street Called "Through"	page	33
Day 6 Poetry Lessons of Time	page	37
Day 7 Embracing Time	page	43
Day 8 Faith in the Fog	page	47
Day 9 Letting Go but Hold Onto the Memories	page	51
Day 10 The Position of Proper Perspective	page	57
Day 11 Celebrate Small Victories	page	63
Day 12 Why Am I So ANGRY?	page	67
Day 13 Beauty of the Brokenhearted	page	73
Day 14 What's Next?	page	77
Day 15 When the Tears Just Won't Stop	page	81
Day 16 Hang On; Pain Ends - HOPE	page	85
Day 17 Grief Does Not Have Me; I Have Grief	page	89
Day 18 God Wired Me That Way	page	95
Day 19 Hidden Pain	page	99
Day 20 Don't Give Up!	page	103
Day 21 Lead Me in Your Path	page	107
Day 22 Guilt or Regret	page	111
Day 23 Lean Into the Pain… Lean Into the Grief	page	117
Day 24 R.E.S.T	page	123
Day 25 Healing in Stillness	page	127
Day 26 His Hands; His Heart	page	133
Day 27 Never Can Say Goodbye	page	137
Day 28 Self-Care	page	143
Day 29 You Shall Live and Not Die	page	149
Day 30 A Stranger in a Strange Land	page	155
Bibliography/Source	page	159
About the Author	page	160
Endnotes	page	162

Grief is the price we
pay for love.

~Queen Elizabeth II~

~REALITY: LOSING OUR SUPERMAN~

"OK, am I dreaming, or is this just Deja Vu? Who are all these people, and who is in this casket?" Then reality hit me and punched me in the middle of my stomach! Oh My God, it's my husband! Wait! Wasn't I just sitting in this same church only a week ago, at the exact same time for the funeral of my sister, Gloria? Wasn't I sitting on this same green cushioned chair, precisely in this spot last week?

I looked down at my feet as I sat staring intensely at this particular mark on the carpet, where it looked like someone may have spilled one or two drops of grape juice used for communion. Then it hit me that it was the same spot I saw a week ago! The tiny stain on the carpet jolted me into realizing that I was at the funeral of my husband, my friend, my lover, and my partner.

The rays of the sun shined through the windows as I sat gazing blankly at the white casket that was draped so elegantly with beautiful petals of red and yellow roses. I knew a portion of my very soul, and a part of the essence of who I was is now lying in the casket with him. On the inside, I could hear myself screaming, "Get up Raymond! Raymond, please get up!" I could feel my inner self wailing uncontrollably. It was like a resounding echo in a valley where nothing existed but the screams of my voice repeatedly shouting, "PLEASE GET UP!" I was hoping this was just a horrible nightmare, but it was not.

God, this is not funny; this feels like such a cruel joke! Father, did I not just bury my sister last week, and now I'm burying my husband this week? But God, we had plans! Remember, we were going to renew our vows? Remember, we had our vacation planned? But it was not a joke; it was real. Yet, I was sitting in the same cushioned chair, composed with the excruciating realization that I am about to bury my husband, my love.

The painful awareness tormented me with each breath that I inhaled and exhaled. I repeated over and over in my head, "You can do this Sherry, you can do this," as I politely smiled upon receiving hundreds of hugs of sympathy and condolences. I rested my back against the chair, trying to ease the tension. I tried to listen to all the kind and loving words spoken about my husband, but everything was fuzzy and sounded so muddled.

In my mind, I was reliving the first day I met him. I still remember the day my uncle Mickey found me, my mom, and my grandmother in a nearby department store. We were sitting at the store's canteen eating lunch when he introduced his friend to us. After brief introductions and minor conversation, my uncle gave us hugs and kisses as usual. And just as quickly as they appeared, he and his friend left smiling and waving.

My grandmother immediately turned to me with "that look" whenever she was about to share something she believed God had spoken to her. It was the look that made you say to yourself, "Oh my God, now what?" She turned to me and said, "See that young man with your uncle right there? He is going to be your husband!" Now you must realize there are four factors to consider in this.

1. I did not know this boy.
2. My parents did not know him.
3. My father would never allow him within a mile of our home, not with his five girls. My father did not play that at all.
4. Last, I was only about 13 or 14 years old at the time, and if I can recall, that young man was about 21 or 22 years old! Now, those numbers do NOT match up no matter how you add or subtract them… it was not happening!

My initial thought was that Nannie really missed God this time, but she did not.

Ten years later, the young man my uncle introduced me to that day, was standing in my parents' home amongst family and friends getting ready to marry me. I recalled feeling I was the luckiest woman on earth that day, and a slight smile escaped my lips. Our 45 years together produced four wonderful children, four grandchildren, and four great-grandchildren. God truly blessed us.

The music from the organ brought me back to reality. So here lies the love of my life, my rock, and my support. I'm sitting here before his casket, utterly empty and void. All I had of my husband was the enormous hole his death left within my heart and soul. I sat there, feeling as though my life has now become nothing but a massive collection of jumbled puzzle pieces.

The frustration arises from not knowing how or if I would put my life back together again because I knew it would never be the same. My thoughts raced and flooded my mind as tears started to flow once again. The picture of my life will never be complete without him because he will always be the missing piece of my puzzle.

No more chasing the sunrise in the mornings. No more dreaming together and sharing funny stories. No more holding hands with each other and listening to our favorite soulful melodies on the radio like we were teenagers. We will no longer watch the sunset over the Chesapeake Bay of Jonas Green Park. Those few minutes of reminiscing shifted my reality to the pain I now see in our children's eyes as they rose and made their way to the final viewing of their dad. Although somewhat shaken and unsteady, I carefully leaned on my oldest son as we all approached the casket… my husband's bed of rest.

My children and I meticulously affixed an emblem of Superman to the top of their dad's casket. I could no longer feel my heart beating. It was as if my heart decided to stop as I leaned in to kiss him goodbye for one last time. I left one final teardrop on his cheek as I gently covered him with the veil. A piece of my heart remains in his casket to this very day. He truly was our Superman.

I miss you the most at night
when everything is quiet and the silence
reminds me that I am not sleeping
next to you.
~Anonymous~

~THE DAY I WILL NEVER FORGET~

I never envisioned waking up thinking this is the last day I will be with the one I love. On a bright and breezy day, I felt like there was a massive cloud over my head as I dragged myself out of bed. I had just buried my sister the day before, and now I had an obligation to get myself together to put on The Annual Spring Health Expo for the county.

I sat on the edge of the bed feeling overwhelmed and wishing I had not committed to facilitating the expo. However, our organization was obligated to the community to execute this annual event. I just sat there for what seemed like an eternity while thinking about the great times I had with my sister. I began to reminisce about her and loved teasing and laughing at her smart and witty comebacks. Suddenly, the tears began to roll down my face uncontrollably.

I started encouraging myself with one of my favorite morning mantras, "Sherry, you can do all things through Christ who gives you the strength, so get it together girlfriend, because you have a lot to do today." Somehow, I thought these words would work for me, but they did not stop the pain.

I began to wonder where in the world was my husband. His usual routine was to wake me with a kiss and say, "I'm on my way out, and I put a breakfast sandwich and coffee by the bed for you." But this morning was different. I missed him waking me with a kiss; my coffee and bag were beside the nightstand. He probably knew how tired I was from preparing for the funeral and how much my sister's death took a toll on me. My husband just wanted me to sleep in; he would often do that. He would not allow anyone to disturb me if I was exhausted, sick or resting… no one! It was his papa bear way of protecting me. So, I got up and prepared for the event. I had to get to the location as my staff was awaiting me. Upon my arrival, I suddenly became terribly ill.

My heart began to palpitate. I could not breathe or move at all. I felt sick in my stomach and thought I was going to pass out. I was so weak as though life had just drained from my body. One of my staff offered to drive me home, but I told him it wasn't necessary. I wanted to try to get home by myself. My best friend called and said she was on her way to help with the event. I told her not to come because I felt ill and was on my way home to lie down. About 15 minutes into my route, my nephew called. He was at my sister's home and needed me to stop by. I told him I was feeling ill and had to get home to lie down.

My initial thought was to go to the hospital, but I quickly changed my mind. Although my heart was racing and aching, I did not want my time consumed with all the tests they would require me to take. I told him to give me some time, and I will be there. As I arrived, I saw the police cars. I just knew it! Someone broke into my sister's home!

We just had her funeral yesterday, and no one was there to monitor the house. I became furious as I got out of my car. I went into the house, and everyone was there, including two police officers. I'm thinking to myself, "What did the thieves take?"

The officer looked at me and asked me if I was Sherry Medley, and I said, "yes." Then he asked me, "Do you know Raymond Medley?" All I can remember is hearing myself screaming endlessly and I just could not stop. I instantly knew at that moment before they spoke another word, that my husband was gone.

My very being spiraled downward into a dark abyss that I never knew existed on earth but has now become a part of my reality. A dark hole of endless pain and torment just opened and completely swallowed me. At this moment, I did not associate my sudden illness aligning with the timing of my husband's death. A few hours later, I realized my illness was connected to my husband as he was leaving me to transition to heaven. For a part of my soul could feel his transition and I felt a part of me left with him.

Several weeks later, God ministered to me that once my husband and I became one, our souls were connected with a covenant of love in the very presence of (and sanctioned by) God. For it was the Lord who had to cut the covenant cord (of over 40 years) between our souls; and my God, it was painful.

Words cannot express the pain I endured with our souls disconnecting and missing the other part of its existence. I can remember the policeman leading me and my daughter, Joy, to his body that was still lying on the marble floor of the church. As we knelt beside his body, we could see the smile and a glow of peace imprinted upon his face. I genuinely believe he saw God in his passing. The Lord assured me through my husband's smile that His son is with Him now.

I must be authentic and transparent, or all my efforts to help others heal will be for naught. I became deeply depressed with suicidal thoughts, was hospitalized for an overdose (miscalculation of medications) and placed on antidepressants to help me get through the days ahead. I praise God for my children, family, friends and pastor who held me up in prayer during this time.

I could not do anything worthy of caring for myself. I went to counseling and grief groups. For six weeks, I laid in my bed in a fetal position without eating and barely drinking. I couldn't talk and felt like I was in a catatonic state. My family and children were so fearful of my mental frame of mind and health. It took me six weeks before I could barely gather enough strength to get out of bed.

Four months later, I was finally able to leave the house, and six months passed before I could be in the presence of family or friends. I could no longer continue operating my business, which I had built with great success. Many things fell to the ground, so I decided to transfer its operation in the hands of a friend. It took me nearly 4 years to get back to reorganizing my business from the ground floor up. I didn't return to church for a whole year.

When I say my life was in turmoil, believe me, it was beyond turmoil. I truly thank God for bringing me through my tragedy. Without a doubt, it was His love that rescued and cradled me in a fetal position. I know what it means to feel His angels encamped around me while protecting me from myself and the hands of the enemy.

I am so grateful for the abundance of God's mercy and grace he extended towards me. Yet, for some reason, I became so ashamed of how messed up I was. I felt I let God down when I experienced my breakdown and no longer wanted to live. I still remember receiving a text from my mentor pastor, asking me how I was doing. I kept her text message as a portion of my strength even to this day.

Pastor Karen: "Good Morning, Sherry. I'm just checking in

on you to see how you are doing."

Me: "Thanks so much; I'm a strong woman, but this has bought me to my knees that I can barely stand. I know about life and death. I love God with everything in me, but I do not understand why this has gripped my soul with so much pain."

Pastor Karen: "This doesn't have anything to do with how strong you are or the strength of your faith and trust in God. The grief that you are experiencing is natural and expected. It doesn't diminish our faith in God. So, don't question your love for God according to your grief. Your grief shows what you have learned from God. You learned how to love, honor, and respect your husband. Your grief is not a dishonor, but evidence of your deep love for your husband."

That was the first and most reviving word I received from another widow who understood where I was at the time. It was like a lifeline to my soul. I lied in bed, and I would literally cry and recite a particular scripture at least a hundred times a day, "Nothing shall separate me from the love of God." I no longer carried boxes of tissues to bed because they could not hold all my tears. I would take a towel to bed each night and find it still saturated with my tears in the morning. I never knew the soul could hold such a reservoir where our tears lingered and flowed.

One thing I cannot even begin to explain is how a part of me was searching for my other half. I felt my soul wandering, searching, crying, and looking for the other part of itself that was missing. My body ached with every breath I took. I felt as though I was suffocating and could not breathe or even catch my breath at times. My existence reminded me of who I wasn't without him. It felt like I was roaming around like a lost child in a maze with no way out. I had lost a part of myself and could not comprehend what was going on within me. What was this indescribable emptiness I was experiencing? Am I crazy or losing my mind?

Yes, I was a real disaster, and no matter how hard I tried to get it together, the struggle was unbearable. Additionally, I wasn't able to find a women's group that could minister to me about this type of pain. I joined a couple of grief counseling programs, but the attendance was not helpful for me. I felt I had no one to pull me aside to advise me of my pain. The excruciating internal ache could not be consoled or healed.

As time passed, with countless prayers and laying before my Father; God, in His infinite wisdom, woke me one night and told me to start writing. Two years later, He instructed me to establish a support group for widows. Someone once wrote that we see God the clearest during our most difficult times, which became the birthing of "Grace for the Journey."

~God's Call for The Journey~

I believe God instructed me to begin Grace for the Journey through my desire to ensure other widows will not feel alone during their life-changing experience. I want to establish a safe place for women seeking emotional and spiritual support from other women who can identify with their pain. I do not want them to feel hopeless and unable to connect with someone who could relate to their grief and sorrow. I want to assist widows through their healing quest with the love of sisterhood, even if it meant me reliving my own pain in order for them to get through their pain.

My book has stories and scenarios; some humorous and some sad. I wanted to share my heart and story of how I was able to travel on this journey called Grief. The process entails some of the questions and activities I utilized during my alone time with God. If you work the pages of each chapter and face all of your emotions (your fears, pain, disappointments, anger, regret, and guilt), I truly believe you will be in a better place to deal with your grief.

Read and meditate on the prayers daily, find something to be grateful for, and share how each chapter relates to your life, spirit and soul. I do not believe I will ever stop grieving the loss of my husband; however, grief will not have power over me; I will have power over grief.

I pray you will dedicate the next 30 days of your journey towards your healing. Healing is an ongoing process until God places you where He needs you to be. Notice, I said "toward" your healing because 30 days is nothing compared to a lifetime of the love you had for your husband. It is the beginning of where God wants to take you to realize that there is purpose in your pain. Rest assured, you will come out more powerful, stronger and more courageous than you can ever imagine. I pray this will be a journey you will take and commit to as you go through your healing process.

I highly recommend the following ideas you can use to get

the most out of the initial 30-day period as you dive into your Devotional Journal:

1. Set aside 15-20 minutes daily to dedicate time toward your healing process.
2. Use your bible if you like to read the scriptures that are provided.
3. Be open to God as you read the daily prayers.
4. Reflect on how each chapter related to your spirit and soul.
5. Use a highlighter and pen and mark up the book; it's your private thoughts.
6. Be ready to take notes of any nuggets or instructions God may give you.
7. Be authentic and transparent with yourself and be truthful with your answers.
8. Prepare your heart to hear what God is saying to you as He guides you with His loving hands toward your healing.
9. Write about why you are grateful. It will help you get through the pain.
10. Be gentle with yourself and take all the time you need. It may be a 30- Day Journal to some, and to others, it may be 90 days. You are walking this journey with God.

As you take this journey, know I am praying for you and that you are not alone. God is with you every step of the way, and He has you in the center of His hands. Be blessed, Sisters.

DAY 1
She is Courageous

Psalms 31:24 NLT
So be strong and courageous, all you who put your hope in the LORD!

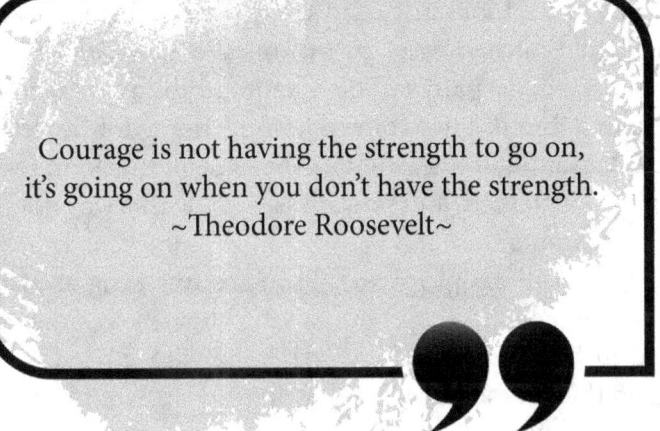

Courage is not having the strength to go on, it's going on when you don't have the strength.
~Theodore Roosevelt~

If you are reading this, then you are wearing "A Robe of Courage" and a "Crown of Bravery." I know it may not feel like it, but you are. I embrace the heroism in you and want you know that you have stepped into a place called "Courageousness." When we look at the meaning of courageous, it is to have the mental or moral strength to venture, persevere, and withstand danger, fear, or difficulty. WOW! Does that sound like "YOU?"

In other words, "Despite the dangers, fear and difficulties, I'm going to use every part of my mind, body and soul to defeat whatever is in opposition to my spirit and conquer what comes against me."

When we decide to take on the struggle and challenges of working through our grieving experience, we have stepped into becoming courageous. I can attest there are times when your bravery is challenged while dealing with the multitude of complexities that fear attempts to generate and circulate. A widow will initially find themselves in an unknown place in their life after their spouse has passed. It takes a tremendous amount of courage to secure enough energy and strength to face grief.

We often find that the people we love may want to protect us from the experience of life's difficulties that accompanies grief. Their thoughts for us to avoid the pain is to stay busy, consider abstract tasks, uncomplicated activities, or conversations.

Most people find it uncomfortable to speak to a loved one about facing grief. How do we look at grief? Do we have the courage to face it? Do we look at it head-on or with peripheral vision? Grief brought me to the lowest part of my life and took me into a place of depression, despair, and devastation. I didn't want to face grief. I hid from it and did not come out of my home for months as though grief was waiting for me on the other side of the door. Even though I felt pitiful, petrified, and powerless, I knew this was not the life God planned for me.

I still recall people saying, "You are so strong and courageous," as I wondered who they were talking about. I was the woman who stayed in bed for weeks. I was the one whose friends would leave food on the doorsteps many mornings so she would have something to eat. I hid under blankets in a fetal position and literally moaned all day. I never saw myself as courageous until one day; God showed me His meaning of the word.

Courageous means having enough strength to trust God by putting one foot in front of the other. God encourages us and tells us in His word:

2 Corinthians 12:9 ESV - "My grace is sufficient for you, for my power is made perfect in weakness. Therefore, I will boast all the more gladly about My weaknesses, so that the power of Christ may rest upon me."

Joshua 1:9 ESV - Have I not commanded you? Be strong and courageous. Do not be frightened, and do not be dismayed, for the LORD your God is with you wherever you go."

<u>Psalms 29:11 ESV</u> – "May the Lord give strength to His people! May the Lord bless His people with peace!"

Commit to a goal of taking one step, no matter what it looks like. Courage doesn't mean you have to do something astronomical or substantial. God's courageousness means you are trusting Him in every decision you make. You may not be able to measure the steps you've already taken or how far you have come. You are more courageous than you think, so celebrate and embrace every milestone you accomplish. We cannot allow the characteristics of grief to prevent us from persevering and pushing through our hurts and disappointments. In the quietness of our soul, we may wrestle with fear, but we will not allow fear to overtake us.

I remember seeing an acronym for FEAR, "Face Everything And Rise."

Let us make a decision to rise up, stare fear in the face and say, "I know I can do this." Guess what? All it took was your "COURAGE!" Ladies, we are resilient, intuitive, strong, phenomenal, secure, and yes… courageous! It is my prayer, as you are reading this book, that your bravery is gaining strength! Congratulations on your medal of COURAGE, and may you wear it always!

1. Have you ever thought of yourself as being courageous?

2. After reading this section, can you identify with being courageous in the earlier stages of grief? Yes? No? and Why?
   _____
   _____
   _____

3. What experiences required you to be courageous during your grief journey?
   _____
   _____
   _____

4. What are the growth steps you would consider to increase your courage?
   _____
   _____
   _____

Prayer

Father, I am so honored that You imparted Your power within me during my fear of the unknown and gave me the courage I needed to face grief. Your grace has upheld, cradled, covered, and restored me. Thank You for allowing the power of Christ to arise in my weakness. Amen

Today I am grateful for:

_____
_____
_____

REFLECTIONS OF MY HEART:

_____
_____
_____
_____
_____

DAY 2
God is Our Safe Place

Psalms 4:8 NLT
"In peace, I will lie down and sleep, for You alone, O LORD, will keep me safe."

> There is no right or wrong way to grieve.
> We can grieve in the arms of others.
> We can grieve in solitude.
> We can grieve through tears,
> laughter, meditation, movement or prayer.
> The only rule is that we hold our hearts with the utmost care and allow ourselves the room to feel and the space to heal with no timelines or expectations.
> ~Liz Arch~

It is so good to know you can lay and sleep in the Father's arms because you have His promise that He will keep you safe. During this time in our lives (a time of despair, a feeling of hopelessness, and distress), we need to have the assurance that there is a "Safe Place" we can go to, a place only our Father can provide and grant to us. The word of God tells us in Acts 17:28 KJV, "For in Him we live, and move, and have our being." My God! Is there a safer place than that… to be completely in Him?

God is saying to us that He is our shield, and He has encompassed us in His vessel of love and protection, no matter what we are experiencing at this moment. Yes, we may be going through, but we are still moving in God, striving in Him, and operating daily in Him. Yes, we are still weeping, hurting, and grieving in Him. But our Father, Jehovah Shammah, is right there with us and feels everything we are experiencing. God has built a shield around us to hold us in His shelter of protection and security. Even if we feel He may be absent, we know that He has not left us. He loves us too much.

God is our shield and a place of refuge. When all our emotions attach themselves to grief, He still holds us in the secret, safe place while gently caressing us in His loving arms. A place of abandonment and disconnect can give us the impression that our family and friends may not understand where we are emotionally. Not only do you feel slight abandonment, but you may conclude they are not as supportive or as sensitive as you need them to be at times. You might even feel alone because their timeline suggests that you may be taking too long to go through "The Process of Grief."

Psalms 3:3 NLT says, "But you, O LORD, are a shield around me; you are my glory, the One who held my head high." Notice the word "high," which means to tower. At this moment, some of us can barely lift our heads off the pillow some mornings, but God is assuring us that the day will come when we will tower over grief. Why? Because He said that He is the one who will hold our heads high! Although we may not feel like it right now, we will not only walk with our heads raised, but lifted spirits will reign over our pain.

God says in Genesis 28:15 KJV, "Behold, I am with you and will keep you wherever you go." God "keeping" us means He is carefully watching over us and guarding us. PRAISE HIM! It is such a comfort to know that God is not a God of abandonment. He is not hidden, but He continually watches and guards us. His love engulfs and overtakes us with the assurance that we are in His "Safe Place."

1. Have you ever felt God was hidden from you during your time of grief?

2. Have you ever felt abandoned by your family members and friends?

3. What and when were some of your feelings of abandonment?
   _____
   _____

4. Name one specific time in which God made you feel really safe during your grieving moment. _____
   _____
   _____

Prayer

Father, from the very depths of my heart, I thank You for loving me and shielding me from the full weight that pain and grief could have brought to my soul. Thank You for allowing me to abide under Your shadow of protection and strength. Thank You for Your steadfast love, which has brought peace to the turbulence that once troubled my soul. Thank You, Father, for not hiding Your face from me in my time of need and for being my safe place. Amen

Today I am grateful for:

_____
_____
_____
_____
_____

REFLECTIONS OF THE HEART:

_____
_____
_____
_____

DAY 3
God's Guiding Light

Psalms 43:3 NIV
"Send me Your light and Your faithful care, let them lead me; let them bring me to Your holy mountain, to the place where You dwell."

> Grief is isolating, but it never leaves you alone. In the moments, we wake up crying, the car rides with tears streaming, grief is our companion. When everyone moves on forgetting our loss, grief remembers.
> ~Laura Coward~

In the midst of grieving, it is so hard to see the light in the dark place. My father had five girls, and he was so proud of each one of us. We called ourselves GB (George Brooks) Girls. In all my years, I never heard my father say anything regarding dissatisfaction with having all girls. He never expressed disappointment that he did not have any boys to rough house, fix cars, put worms on fishing hooks, or do the testosterone things fathers and sons would do together.

My father would always proudly proclaim, "I Love My Girls." However, since we did not have any brothers, we had to help our father cut wood, empty the commode pans, haul water, cut grass, etc. My dad was a hard worker and a great provider for the family. He drove the cattle truck from city to city, which caused him to be away from home a lot. I can still see him in his red plaid flannel shirt and blue jeans as he hopped up in the big old shabby truck packed with cattle.

One of the fondest memories I have of my dad was seeing him work on his car during the weekends. As a little girl, I still remember the pinkish, salmon-colored Studebaker he owned. As I knelt beside him, the gritty stones in the yard made indentation into my knees. He instructed me to provide him with a specific wrench by describing the size, shape, and color. I certainly did not know a Phillip screwdriver from an Allen wrench! But I picked it up and asked, "Is this the one, Daddy?" My fingernails would be black from the car grease and oil on the wrenches. My hands were filthy dirty from being on the ground due to pure curiosity of wanting to see what my dad was doing under the car. My mom would have a fit because her daughter looked like a little grease monkey.

I was reminded that I had to be instructed by my earthly father of which tool to utilize to fix a problem. God gives us instructions (tools) on how to move forward in our healing process because he wants us to become whole and healed. He may guide you to connect with a grief support group, counselor, pastor, a physician (for possible medications), or a very good friend to assist you. Be open to the instruments or tools He gives you to consider and allow Him to lead you.

Later in life, I realized my dad really enjoyed knowing I was there with him, even if I had no idea what he was doing. It was not as though he needed "my help," but he knew I wanted to help him and be there in his presence. Just being with my dad made me feel so special because he wanted his little girl right beside him. Can I tell you this thought still brings a smile to my face? I believe it is somewhat of a reflection of how God is with us; He does not need our help but desires us to be in His presence.

As years passed, there were many times in the evenings he needed one of his girls to hold the light so he could see under the hood. Being the oldest, I was usually the one who was chosen for the task. He would even at times place the light in my hand and instruct me to move it in various places to locate the problem. He even gave me the wrench and told me how to use it as he held the light. The closer I got to my natural father, the more he was able to show me where the problem was that caused the car not to operate correctly.

As I began to think on this, it so parallel with the fact that there are times we must get very close to our heavenly Father. We must allow His presence, the light of His Spirit and His word to take up residence in us as He guides us in moving forward.

The closer we are to God, the more He desires to guide us through our dark places and repair our mindset. Even in grief, we must do the work to move toward healing, which can be very painful and challenging. Sometimes the level of effort can feel like it's a dirty job and so unfair.

During my grief period, it was difficult to connect with what God was doing, but I had to trust the truth of who God is. I didn't know how He was going to fix the brokenness of my soul and spirit. I needed HELP! I literally thought I was going to lose my mind because I had already lost who I use to be when I lost the love of my life. But I knew God allowed me to hold onto "His Light" and His word as He continually guided me through the place of pain and grief, and shifted my focus toward healing.

1. When were you in your darkest place? _____
   _____
   _____

2. When you view the light of God in the midst of your grief, how has His light brought you closer to Him?_____
   _____
   _____

3. When was the moment you remembered the illumination of God bringing you to a place of inner peace during your grief?
   _____
   _____
   _____

Prayer

Father, thank You for Your guiding light which has placed me on a path to overcome the pain and grief that hindered me and created a very dark place within my thoughts. Allow me to see Your light of illumination within my soul and abide in Your holy place to dwell in Your peace. Thank You for Your light, love, and healing power of Jesus Christ. Amen

Today I am grateful for:

_____
_____
_____
_____

REFLECTIONS FROM MY HEART:

_____
_____
_____
_____
_____
_____

DAY 4
From Trauma to Trust to Triumph

Psalms 84:12 KJV
"O LORD of host, blessed is the man who trusts in You!"

> Some of us have been through things so traumatic that the human mind isn't built to handle, but we fight and persevere every single day and night. If that's not strength, I don't know what is. You are a survivor.
> ~Unknown~

Life can break you. I could not understand what I was going through physically, mentally, or emotionally. And now, I was also fighting a spiritual attack. I was literally fighting for my life while battling for physical strength, mental existence, and spiritual survival. This warfare was real! The enemy wanted my mind, and I had to establish perimeters against him in order to bring every thought into captivity. As a believer, my trust and faith in God were being challenged like never before.

My tragedy was trying to engulf me with an abyss of fear, pain, and mistrust. In full transparency, it is so hard to trust when you are hurt, heartbroken and wounded. I could not verbalize my thoughts, internal pain, or mental anguish to anyone. There were times that I was unable to focus on who or where I was. I had completely shutdown and was struggling to survive.

When a tragedy takes root, your whole life is filled with a knot full of jumbled emotions; resembling a massive ball of tangled yarn. No matter how hard you try to untwist it, there is no end to the entanglement, and it becomes more and more complicated. You don't know where to begin and end up inheriting frustration. So, what do you do when you don't know what to do? You must trust God. I had to go back in my mind to the last time where God showed up in my life's troubles. I had to shift my focus on the "WHEN" part of God.

The last time:

WHEN He wiped my tears
WHEN He bought me out of a situation
WHEN He worked a miracle for me
WHEN He healed me
WHEN He handled an impossible situation

The memories above were all connected to the remembrance of "WHEN" God did exactly what He said He was going to do. I knew I had to trust the "WHEN" of God. When I think about the word trust, I think about how we feel so honored and privilege when someone says they trust or have faith in us. Imagine how God feels when we completely put our trust in Him. God needs us to lean on Him. It is essential to know that deep down inside of us, there is an eternal trust we have in God, even through our tears. In our tears, we must trust Him and know that we will triumph over our trauma and circumstances.

My husband's death truly challenged my trust in God. I could not comprehend why this tragedy happened. Why didn't God give me a warning, or did He and I did not notice it? Either way, my trust in God was weak as I walked out this ordeal in my life. I am stating this because sometimes we do grow weak and weary no matter how strong we may feel we are. Psalms 73:26 KJV says, "My flesh and my heart may fail, but God is the strength of my heart and my portion forever."

God needs us to relinquish our pain, gently lay it in His loving arms and simply trust Him. He calls us to Himself in the weakness of our hurt and despair. Our tears do not signify a lack of trust in God; they validate our faith to trust Him in the midst of our pain.

At one point, I felt like Job. God, you took my sister, and less than 24 hours after leaving her gravesite, I was told my husband is dead. Then a few months later, my baby sister passed from pancreatic cancer. And a few months after that my best friend lost her husband. I'm sure you can understand that my trust had grown increasingly frail, but like Job (and through my screams and tears), I was able to say what he mentions in scripture. Job 13:15 NKJV reads, "Though He slay me, yet will I trust Him." The Easy English Bible reads, "Even if God kills me, I will still believe in Him."

During my trauma, I begged God to take me; the pain was too heart-crushing. I did not want to live without my husband. But I had to trust God to hold my hand during this time with every bit of conviction I had left. I had to believe all of what I knew of Him. I had to stand on every word I read and the revelational knowledge of who He is and His attributes.

I needed to receive clarity from God as He walked with me on this journey. When I felt so distant from Him, I continued to trust He would draw me closer and bring me to a place of peace during the most traumatic times of my life. Nahum 1:7 NKJV states, "The LORD is good, a stronghold in the day of trouble; And He knows those who trust in Him." When all is said and done, He knew I would trust Him, and so will you.

1. Did your trust in God waiver after your loved one's death?

2. If yes, when did your trust in God become restored?

3. What specifically happened that caused your trust to return?
   _____
   _____
   _____

4. What are you trusting God for during this time in your life?
   _____
   _____
   _____

5. Write a prayer and tell the Lord what you are trusting Him for.
   _____
   _____
   _____
   _____
   _____

Prayer

Father, the words I speak from my heart to Your heart is, "I TRUST YOU, GOD!" I know You are right here with me, and You're aware of everything I'm going through. Lord, You are good, powerful, and strong. You told me to trust You and not to lean on my own understanding. I know I can stand on Your word, for it shall never return to You void. Father, I am trusting and embracing Your love towards me, always. Amen

Today I am grateful for:

_____
_____
_____
_____

REFLECTIONS OF MY HEART:

_____
_____
_____
_____
_____
_____

DAY 5
Grief is on a One-Way Street Called "Through"

Psalms: 23:4 NIV
"Even though I walk through the darkest valley, I will fear no evil, for you are with me; your rod and your staff, they comfort me."

> You don't get over it,
> you just get through it.
> You don't get by it,
> because you can't get around it.
> It doesn't "get better,"
> it just gets different.
> Every day, grief puts on a new face.
> ~Gay Hendericks~

My mind takes me back to when I was 5 or 6 years old and we would sing a song while playing a particular game. Everyone would hold hands in a circle and one person would be in the middle of that circle and try to break through it at the end of the song. I only knew a few stanzas of the song, but the lyrics were, "You can't go over it, you can't go under it, you can't go around it, you must go through it." I remember when it got to the part of going through it, we would almost whisper it; fearful that whatever we had to go through did not catch us. It's funny how 60 years later, those words are still vividly etched in my mind. I would try to run through my friends without getting caught but was always unsuccessful after repeated attempts.

I believe tackling grief requires the same mindset. You can't go around grief. You can't go over it or under it; you must go through it. There is no cure for grief; you cannot run from it, hide from it, ignore it, or turn your back on it. You must face it head-on, face to face, stare it in the eyes, and let it know, "You might hold me in your grip, and it may take a while, but I am going to make it through my pain." We cannot immerse ourselves into being so busy that we create a falsehood which we have dealt with our grief.

Grief needs to be acknowledged because it's a part of you. It is intertwined with the love you have for your husband and all of your inner feelings combined. We generally grieve the hardest for the ones we love the most. In our grief, we are honoring the loss of our loved one. When we are grieving, we feel like we are walking through "Death's Darkest Valley," but God tells us that we should not fear; for He is with us, and the Holy Spirit is our comforter. Grief is a "part" of life, but we do not have to allow it to "become" our life.

My best friend, Valerie lost her husband not long after I lost mine. His death devastated me to the core, so naturally after our husband's death we were one another's support system. The four of us were more like family than two married couples for I have always considered her to be my sister and him like a brother. Valerie is a very energetic, athletic, avid runner and aerobics fitness instructor. She is such a wonderful person, and I fondly consider her free-spirited and very spontaneous. After her husband passed, Valerie expressed the need to talk and be around people. She also shared how running burned energy and released endorphins, which allowed her to keep her mind clear of her grief, especially on her most difficult days.

Valerie had to find a way to take her mind off the pain. I recall telling her, "Just when you feel you have widened the gap against grief, it is standing at the finish line saying, "So, you thought you could outrun me, huh? No one can outrun me!" There are no shortcuts, gimmicks, or quick fixes with grief. If it were so, I would have spent every dime to stop or remove the pain I had to endure. Grief is a difficult journey; however, we can and will make it "through."

1. Can you remember the darkest day you had with grief?

2. How did you handle it?

   _____
   _____
   _____
   _____

3. What were your thoughts during that time?

   _____
   _____
   _____

4. Have you ever tried to run from grief by ignoring it?

5. What are some of the things you did to keep your mind off grief?

   _____
   _____
   _____

Prayer

Father, I am so grateful and honored for the intimacy of Your presence in my life. I know I am grieving the one I deeply love, and I honor him through my grieving period. Although I may be in a dark place, I know You are with me. You will never leave me because Your love is here to comfort me in the empty space he once occupied. Amen

Today I am grateful for:
_____
_____
_____
_____

REFLECTIONS FROM THE HEART:
_____
_____
_____
_____
_____

DAY 6
WHO IS TIME?
WHAT IS TIME?
WHERE IS TIME?

Psalms 90:12 KJV
"So, teach us to number our days, that we may gain a heart of wisdom."

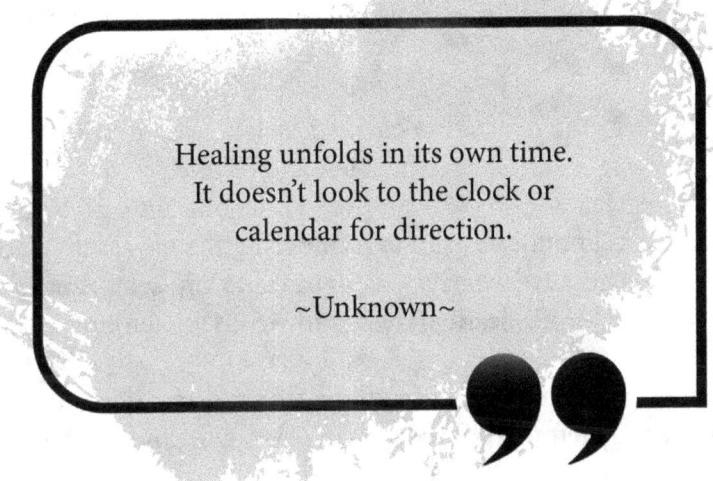

Healing unfolds in its own time.
It doesn't look to the clock or
calendar for direction.

~Unknown~

Who is Time? What is Time? Where is Time?
by Sherry Medley

We have heard the old adages, "Time heals all wounds",
"Give it Time", "Time waits for no one", "We should never waste Time."

My mind began to wonder; then I started realizing that
you cannot get Time back, pray Time will come back,
hope Time will return back,
or pay to get Time back.

You cannot hold Time or put Time in a cage.
You cannot recapture Time or make up Time.
Time never returns. Time never looks back.

Nothing can make up for lost Time; once Time leaves, it is never there again.
Therefore, Time is so precious. It lasts only for a moment, then it is gone forever.

Only the sun, moon and stars can measure Time in the elements of the past, present and future.
Lost Time evolves into memories; it then becomes "I remember when."
Death brings a reality to Time; it brings the clarity of the importance of Time.

It brings the realization of the pricelessness, invaluableness, and exquisiteness of Time.
Death has no power over Time, but Time gracefully relinquishes itself to numbering the days unto God.
I say this because we never seem to value and see the beauty of Time until death arrives, and we no longer have it.

Yes, we think Time was stolen away from us, or did we just give it away?
We are only left with the regrets of wasting it, and not handling it with the loving care given to us. Yes… this thing we call Time.

So why do we waste such a precious gift as that of Time, never realizing its value until death comes and snatches it away from us?

Time has given its heart to us, but we have abused and ignored it, and set it aside for another Time, all because we always believed we have plenty of it.
So, we try to find Time only to realize that death has come to proclaim its rights from us upon this earth but not from eternity.

Time is so pure, one of the purest things in the universe.
Time can only be used once, it cannot be recycled.
So we cannot bully Time into staying longer than it should, but we can benefit from its presence.

It cannot be exploited, but it can be meaningful and mastered.
It cannot be manipulated, but it can be mindfully managed.
It cannot be changed, but it can be handled carefully.
It cannot stand still, but as it moves, you can savor the blessings of it.
It can be hated, but Time can also bring healing.

You cannot coerce Time but in Time it can bring comfort, clarity, and contentment.
Time is consistent and predictable,
yet we are unpredictable and inconsistent with Time.

Time has always been there for us, it is dependable and works hand in hand with faith.
Yet, we are not faithful to Time.
Time is to be celebrated, applauded, honored, and cherished.
Time doesn't look to be worshipped or idolized but to be respected.
Time can birth abundance and greatness into the world.

It is to be appreciated and valued,
because Time is so amazing with what it can accomplish.
God has blessed us with Time. Time to reap, Time to sow,
Time to pluck up.
God gave us a Time in every season of our lives.

Time can birth dreams and visions.
Time can empower and strengthen.
Time can forgive and bring freedom.
Time can produce growth, greatness, and gratefulness.
Time can bring hope, humility, and humbleness.
In Time there is love, laughter and joy.
So, with this thing call Time,
we must respect and cherish every moment of it.
For we never know when it's our Time.

I intentional repeated Time in this piece of poetry so we can understand the value and the working of Time. After reading the poetry, there are some excerpts in which you can circle below all that best describes your grief journey or life experiences with Time. Write how it has been applied to your life personally.

1. Time cannot be exploited but can be meaningful and mastered.
2. Time cannot be manipulated but can be managed and mishandled.
3. Time cannot be changed but can be handled carefully.
4. Time does not stand still.
5. Time can be hated but can also bring healing.
6. Time can bring comfort, clarity, and contentment.
7. Time is consistent and predictable.
8. Time has always been there for you.
9. Time is dependable and works hand in hand with faith,
10. Time is to be celebrated, applauded, honored, and cherished.
11. Time is to be respected.
12. Time can birth abundance and greatness into the world.
13. Time is blessed by God.
14. Time can birth dreams and visions.
15. Time can empower and strengthen.
16. Time can forgive and bring freedom.
17. Time can produce growth, greatness, and gratefulness.
18. Time can bring hope, humility, and humbleness.
19. Time has shown me my seasons on how to plant, sow and reap.
20. Time is something that I now have a different view.

Prayer

Father, teach me to walk in wisdom so I can redeem the time which has been assigned to me. Father, I believe You have given me a measure of Time. It is up to me as Your child to utilize the Time given to me to Your glory. Thank You for the grace and mercy You have given to me today, as I walk hand in hand with You for you are the creator of Time and hold it in Your hands.

Today I am grateful for:
_____
_____
_____

REFLECTIONS FROM THE HEART:
_____
_____
_____

DAY 7
Embracing Time

Psalms 31:15a NIV
"My times are in your hands;"

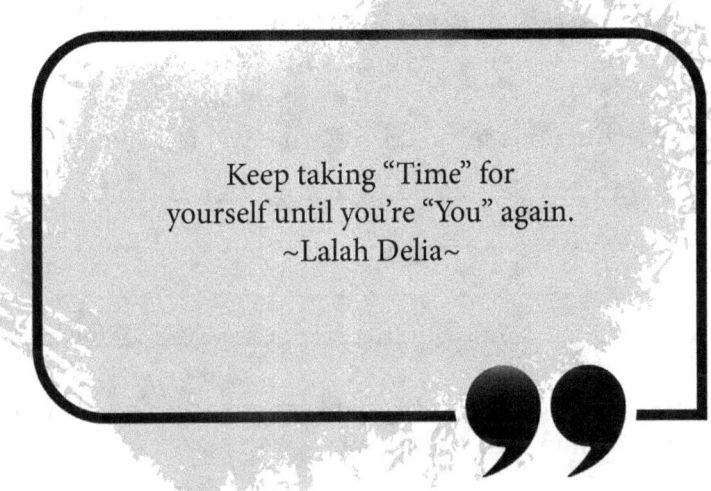

Keep taking "Time" for
yourself until you're "You" again.
~Lalah Delia~

After my husband's transition, all I had was TIME. I needed and depended on time. My mind goes back to when I thought that we didn't have enough time, but in reality, we really did.

Life is only as important as you make it, but nothing is more important than living your best life with the time that has been given to you. Yes, your heart does grieve after the loss of a loved one, but you cannot stop living. Time has not become your enemy, but your ally. It will take time to heal, adjust, grow into a stronger person, and move forward. Time is needed to begin to accept the fact that, "No, he is not coming back." It's going to give you the solace of knowing that in time, you both will be together with God one day.

Grief, death, and time have taught all of us to value life and people to the fullest. Please allow "time" to comfort and caress you, hold you tight, and process where you are as you walk out the next part of your journey. Grief is not your enemy, so please do not rush it or fight it. Take all the time you need to grieve. Allow time to carry you through this journey. Grief does not carry time… time carries grief. God is Omnipresent and He is time. Allow God to heal you and your heart in His time. Embrace the beauty of time amid your grief, hold it close to your heart, and give it out to those you love. Cherish the memories of the time you had with your husband.

Rick Warren once wrote, "Time is your most precious gift because you only have a set amount of it."[1] We need to value the gift of the set amount of time God has given us.

1) After reading this section, write what you feel about time.

_____
_____
_____
_____

2) What are some of the things you experienced and plan to change regarding the importance of time?

_____
_____
_____
_____

3) Write three things you have procrastinated about in the past but will move forward to accomplish: Example: School, visiting someone special, vacation adventure, purchasing something specific, work on your bucket list, etc.

_____
_____
_____
_____

Prayer

Father, thank You for the time You have generously given me while on this earth. I shall not waste it but treat it as a precious jewel. I will not squander it, but vow to use it to Your glory and spread the love of Jesus with every second that You have given me. God, I thank You for renewing, reviving, and restoring me during this season of my life. Amen

Today I am grateful for:

_____
_____
_____
_____

REFLECTIONS OF THE HEART:

_____
_____
_____
_____

DAY 8
Faith in the Fog

Psalms 18:28 NASB
"For You light my lamp; The LORD my God illumines my darkness."

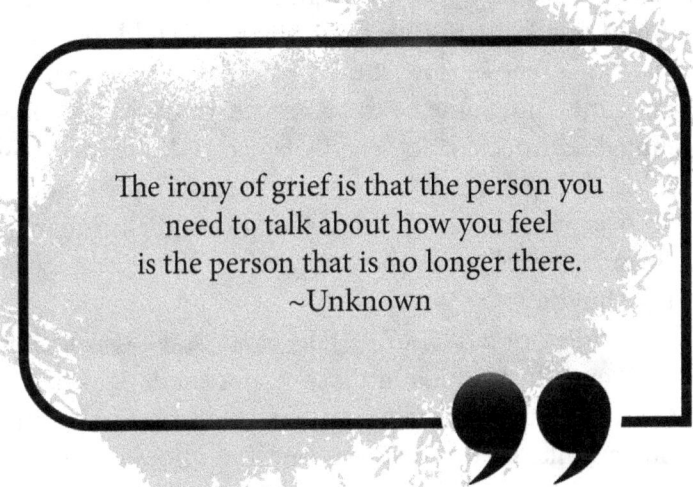

> The irony of grief is that the person you need to talk about how you feel is the person that is no longer there.
> ~Unknown

I always looked forward to taking our daughter back to college. The drive took us through the beautiful mountains of Western Maryland. However, during this one particular trip, my husband and I ran into a massive blanket of dense fog. I was startled that it came upon us so quickly and totally out of nowhere. The moment reminded me of life. There are times when the beauty of life can be going so well, and out of nowhere, the misfortunes of life's situations and circumstances are ever-present. We continued to drive but could barely see the cars in front of us. I suggested to my husband that maybe we should pull over until it lifted. At this time, fear had stepped in and I was literally petrified. We could barely see the hood of the car, and my heart was beating like crazy!

My husband could tell I was scared to death. Then I remembered him saying with such reassurance, confidence, and calmness (which was a part of his personality), "Babe, it's safer to go through it slowly than to stop in the middle of it." He would always tell me that stopping in the middle of heavy fog could cause more damage than going through it slowly at your own pace (and with warning flashers on). He would add, "Never, pay attention to how fast others are driving; go at the pace that's comfortable to you."

"Widow's Fog" is very real and similar to a physical fog. You "see" life and are walking "through" life, but your thoughts and surroundings feel foggy to you right now. I believe those who have lost a loved one (whether it's their husband, child, parent or wife), walk through a type of "fog" during grief. It is in these times that we must keep moving. Some of the characteristics of a "Widow's Fog" are feeling disconnected, detached, disoriented, and disengaged. You are unable to organize or reorganize your thoughts, and a simple task can overwhelm you. Without going into the mechanics, or the medical and psychological operations of the brain, you feel like your brain has shut down.

The mindset of a "Widow's Fog" may leave you feeling overly burdened, out of control, and discombobulated. At times, you may even feel like you are moving in slow motion. Other times, your emotions are like a yo-yo; you are up one moment and down the next.

You feel yourself falling, but you can't stop or even help yourself. The three-pound brain in your body must now organize, decipher, and comprehend life as never before "plus" incorporate what you are currently going through. In other words, you are in an emotional overload. Nothing seems to make sense, and you are in total survival mode while trying to find your way back to that person you once were. You even begin to wonder if that person exists anymore.

Psalms 139:12 NIV states, "Even the darkness will not be dark to you; the night will shine like the day, for darkness is as light to you." What is God saying? No matter how dark life may seem to you, it is not darkness to God, because wherever He is, there will always be light. If we are with Him (even in our darkest moments), we are still traveling in the light of the Father. Therefore, you are never alone, and you will not be in a dark place forever.

You will find your way out of the fog if you just keep moving.

God is there with you and will continually guide you through your journey. Put your trust in the Lord daily, allow Him to navigate you through the fog, and you will come out of it. Your spirit will shine again, and you will find yourself on the other side of the mountain.

Well, as we continued to drive through the mist that day. After a while, I began to see a hint of the sun peeking through the fog. My eyes caught the beautiful multi-colored fall leaves hugging the trees as they stood tall on the mountains. We were finally out of the fog, and the weight of concern I previously felt was lifted. As you begin to move out of your fog, you will feel an essence of relief and realize God is bringing you and your thoughts into a much brighter day.

1. Have you ever felt like you have been in a Widow's Fog?

2. Describe the fogged thoughts you are currently experiencing.

   _____
   _____
   _____

3. How did you feel God guided or ministered to you during your fog?

   _____
   _____
   _____

4. What are some of the things you did or can do to help you through it?

   _____
   _____
   _____

Prayer

Father, I seek Your face and guidance as I maneuver through this time of haziness and confusion. I place my eyes on You, for I know You are with me always. Even though I cannot see what lies ahead, I know You are holding my hand, as the light of Your presence leads me into a place of clarity and peace.

Today I am grateful for:

_____
_____
_____
_____

REFLECTIONS FROM THE HEART:

_____
_____
_____
_____

DAY 9
Letting Go but Hold Onto the Memories

Psalms: 143:5 CEV
"I remember to think about the many things you did in years gone by."

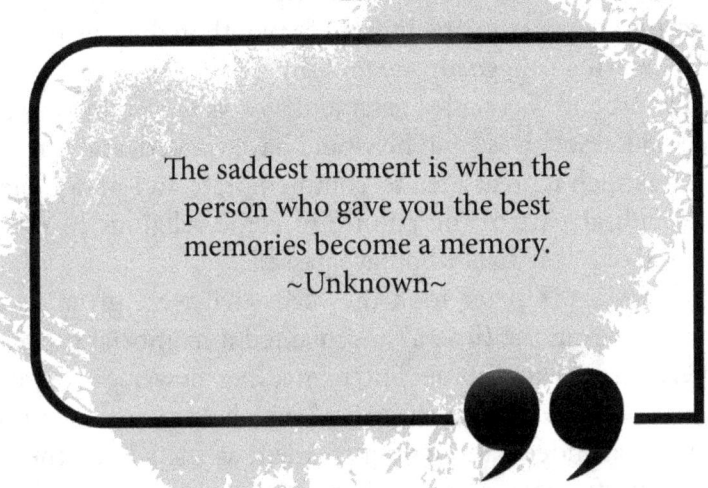

The saddest moment is when the person who gave you the best memories become a memory.
~Unknown~

Moving forward can be challenging at times. After the death of my husband, all I knew was that I never wanted to forget who he was or have his presence ever leave me. It was my desire to always be reminded of the kind, gentle, and giving soul he was. I wanted his love for life, family, and God to always be at the forefront of my mind.

I was so terrified that time would cause me to lose the feeling of his presence or the sound of his voice. I was afraid when the tears slowed down it meant that I might be losing him all over again. I don't ever want to let him go. The song sung by recording artist Danny Gokey, is about a husband who lost his wife early in life. One of his lyrics best describes the feelings regarding the loss of a loved one. The lyrics are, "I don't wanna feel better… I don't wanna not to remember. I will always see your face in the shadow of this haunted place. I will laugh, I will cry, shake my fist at the sky, but I will not say goodbye."[2]

Granted, nothing and no one except God and his love, could or would ever fill this void. I needed to memorialize the memories of my husband without idolizing him. I felt compelled to do something for my inner self to be satisfied; the inner part of me that was so empty without him.

We received monetary donations during the time of the funeral. I spoke with my children and told them that we needed to use the money to set up a scholarship fund for youth in the community who will be entering college for the first time.

My husband was such a giver and always helped those who were in need. I knew this is what he would have wanted, and our children felt it was such a great idea to commemorate and honor their dad. It is a natural part of the culture in some religions to establish a memorial of loved ones who have passed.

My husband's sister took the seeds that were given as gifts in his name during the funeral and planted a memorial garden along the perimeter of her home. She named her flower garden after her brother and called it "Ray's Garden," which was such an appropriate name. It was indeed a touching moment as she shared the pictures of the beautiful flowers surrounding the borders of her home. It was sort of like him saying, "I'm here all around you Sis."

The scripture talks about how God's thoughts are precious to us. Our thoughts are also precious toward our loved ones, and there are many ways we can choose to hold onto those memories. God's thoughts of us are so vast; it would outnumber the sands of the seas. I cannot begin to fathom how much we are in the mind of God every single day.

The Lord knows that the thoughts of our loved ones would never touch the eternal, vast, and infinite thoughts He has for us. Jeremiah 29:11 NKJV says, "For I know the thoughts that I have towards you, says the LORD, thoughts of peace and not evil, to give you a future and a hope." May this scripture open your eyes to God's love for you as you continue to carry the thoughts of your loved one in your heart.

Here are 15 ways to keep those memories tangible as you begin to move forward:

1. <u>Dedicate a Bench</u> - in your local park or even one in your yard.
2. <u>Memorial Garden</u> - Make a beautiful memory with an array of flowers and plants.
3. <u>Donation</u> - Donate to a local organization, charity, or youth program.
4. <u>Plant a tree</u> - One year before my husband passed, he planted a sapling in the yard. After he passed, our family planted a small memorial garden in his name beside our home.
5. <u>Create a Treasured Pillow</u> - I took one of my husband's shirts and made it into a pillow, which I have on my bed and sleep with each night. Additionally, some department stores will engrave pictures and make items for you. Check the web for other memorable ideas.
6. <u>Framed Love</u> - When my grandmother passed, I framed one of her handkerchiefs. You may want to consider this as an option with an item of your loved one.
7. <u>Annual Day</u> - In memory of your loved one, it would be great to have a special get-together with a cook-out, dinner, or dessert, which can be done on a particular day such as their birthday, anniversary, etc.
8. <u>A Jar of Love</u> - I took the flowers from my husband's grave and had them dried and placed in a large mason jar with ribbons of his favorite football team colors. When I enter my home, they are sitting on the tabletop of the stairs as though he is welcoming me home for the day.
9. <u>Scattering of Ashes</u> - You can make the scattering of ashes a small or large event. You may want to spread the ashes at a favorite destination your loved one enjoyed or a location they always wanted to visit. There is also jewelry in which you can place the ashes and wear them daily.
10. <u>Heart of Flowers</u> - Take the flowers from the funeral and put them in a picture frame in the shape of a heart with their name and picture inside.
11. <u>Engraved Frame</u> - My children gave me a beautiful picture frame with our picture in it with one of his favorite quotes engraved in

gold lettering.
12. Picture Collage - In a large picture frame, take an assortment of pictures of your loved one with family and friends and add a quote that best describes them. Examples include "You Are the Greatest," "A Perfect Dad," or "We Love You to the Moon." Be original and have fun with it.
13. A Shadow Box – One of my best friends designed a beautiful, white wooden glass-encased shadow box with pictures of my husband and me, along with scriptures, quotes, small personal items, dried flowers, and trinkets.
14. Build a Bear - If you have an affectionate voicemail or a form of recording, apply it inside a stuffed animal. Consider a voicemail message with "I Love You," etc.
15. Memory Quilt - A memory quilt would be an excellent activity as a family get together project. Use patches of your loved one's shirts or ties to create a quilt. I have seen pocketbooks made out of ties as well as centerpieces.[3]

Allow your imagination to go wild and wide. Read and research through the internet and check out various craft books to find additional ways to memorialize your loved one. If you have children, this will help them with their grief as well.

The internet is a great place to start. Memorable projects are idea ways to help fill a part of the hole you have in your heart. These activities can be done at any time. There is no rush, as grief has its own timeline. You may become a bit emotional working on some of these activities and reminiscing of your time with your loved one. Sensitivity may set in and tears may fall, but there will also be moments of smiles and laughter. You are moving forward, and this is all a part of your healing journey.

1. What are your thoughts on continuing the memory of your husband through a tangible activity?

   _____

   _____

   _____

2. Choose one thing you would like to do to memorialize your husband's memories.

3. If you decide to consider a memory project, make sure to initiate a start and completion date. Remember, you decide when to take on the project, and in your time.

Prayer

Father, I am so grateful that Your love and thoughts towards me are immeasurable and infinite. Thank You for the loving and fond memories You have given me, and for allowing the love of my husband to be forever etched and sealed in my heart as I continue to journey on this road with You. Amen

Today I am grateful for:

_____
_____
_____
_____

REFLECTIONS OF THE HEART

_____
_____
_____
_____
_____

DAY 10
The Position of Proper Perspective

Psalms 100:5 NLT
"For the LORD is good. His unfailing love continues forever, and His faithfulness continues to each generation."

> But grief is a walk alone.
> Others can be there and listen,
> but you will walk alone down your own path,
> at your own pace, with your sheared-off pain,
> your raw wounds, your denial, anger and bitter loss.
> You'll come to your own peace, hopefully.
> But it will be on your own, in your own time.
> ~Cathy Lamb~

During certain times in our lives, we may struggle with putting things into "Proper Perspective." The topic of Proper Perspective may seem a little sensitive, but I can assure you, it is very necessary. I pray you will allow me to convey what God spoke to me with an open heart that I used as a guide through my own steps toward healing. I believe these tools will be helpful to you also.

When a person loses a loved one, things become perplexed and challenging at times. Remember the Widow's Fog experience shared earlier? Moments can feel unreal and somewhat illusionary in our lives. We struggle almost daily to put things in some sort of order because now our former "order" feels completely "Out of Order." And the normalcy we use to experience is no longer normal. Our perspective of life has now become quite muddled and confused.

I remembered begging God daily to please give me my husband

back. After all, He is the "All-Powerful" God. I told Him that He's also Omnipresent and controls time. He could reach back in time and make it the day before my husband passed. Talking about "Not putting things in proper perspective?" That was me! It was so delusional of me to even think or consider that God would do either one of the two. However, I would repeatedly ask Him these questions daily for nearly two years, "Please God, can You give me back my husband?"

When God took my Raymond, I wanted Him to take me also. Does this sound familiar to you? Or have you heard this from someone who's lost a loved one? I still remember standing in the church at the podium, well-poised and articulate in speech as I spoke of the greatness of my husband and the father of our children. My exact words were, "My husband was not just a good man; he was a great man." Yes, he was a great man, and I wanted to share with the world what I knew about him. Although my well-hidden stance expressed one thing, I wanted to lay across his casket and never stop screaming.

When Raymond left me, so much of whom I was left with him. I could not function or even find a purpose in life or a will to live. To reiterate, I couldn't even get out of my bed for over a month. I cried every single day for several months after his passing. I pleaded for God to please take me so I could be "with" my husband because I just could not exist without him.

One day as I was weeping during prayer, God spoke to me in such an empathetic, sweet voice of love, compassion, and gentleness, with a reprimand that still rings within my spirit today. The Lord said, "So, your desire to be with your husband in heaven is more than your desire to be with Me in heaven?" At that time, my heart ached with conviction because I knew wanting to go to heaven to be with my husband was selfish and out of my own needs. My primary desire should be with that of Jesus and not with my husband. It was at that point I realized that I had put my longing for my husband before the longing of Christ. Now, this may seem hard to swallow and accept, but in reality, it's the truth. I had to stop and put things in "Proper Perspective."

During pain, frustration, anger, and grief, we may not realize how much we have lost our perspective of death. I know I unconsciously and unknowingly lost perspective. We may not realize how our thoughts may have shifted during our time of distress, and deep grief can unintentionally change our mental posture. I have been in ministry for over 40 years and in Christ for 55 years. However, the feeling of being grief-stricken clouded my senses, knowledge, and views of death, life, and yes, Jesus.

We must be very careful never to place anything and anyone before our Lord. We cannot allow anything to separate us from the knowledge of God's love, not even the death of our loved one because He is a jealous God. 2 Corinthians 11:2a KJV states, "For I am jealous for you with Godly jealousy."

God loves us so much. He makes emphasis regarding His love and protection for us as widows. The Lord grieves when we grieve, and He weeps when we weep. He captures every single one of our tears in His vase and holds it close to His heart. God shows such tenderness toward us. It is very comforting to know as widows that we are one of the heartbeats of God, and He requires that we are taken care of.

1. Psalms 68:5 NIV states, "A Father to the fatherless, a defender, (protector, guardian, bodyguard) of widows, is God in His holy dwelling."
2. Psalms 146:9a ESV says, "The LORD watches over the sojourners; He upholds the widow and the fatherless…."
3. Exodus 22:22 NIV states, "Do not take advantage of the widow or the fatherless."
4. I Timothy 5:3 KJV says, "Honour (Honor) widows that are widows ."
5. Zechariah 7:10 NKJV states, "Do not oppress the widow or the fatherless."

We are biblically reminded of God's care for us who are now widows. As we struggle and walk through so many changes and storms in our lives, we can see how much God loves and protects widows in His word. God's heart is close to our hearts, but we cannot allow the loss of our loved one to become an idol in our life. My grief and sorrow temporarily blinded me to what I was doing spiritually.

When I opened my eyes after prayer, the truth of where my mindset had drifted stabbed me in my heart and brought tears of repentance to my eyes. I had to ask God for forgiveness of my ignorance while I was in despair. God's tender mercies nudged and admonished me of my error. He did not rebuke or scold me with anger or severity. He drew me closer to His heart and embraced me with His love knowing the depth of my grief, broken heart, and sorrow affected my perspective. Do I still shed tears at times? Yes! Do I still miss my husband? Absolutely! Does my heart still ache? Indeed! Do I yearn to be with him in heaven more than wanting to be with Jesus? No!

God knew with His help that I had to put things in its "Proper Perspective" in order for Him to bring healing. You may ask yourself if healing will ever come. Healing is a process of its own. Everyone heals differently, but healing will come, and one day, you will be able to replace those tears with a smile of the beautiful memories you have of your loved one.

1. Have you ever lost perspective in longing for your husband?

2. How did you respond to losing perspective?

_____

_____

_____

_____

3. After reading how God proclaims His love and protection for you as a widow, how will you gain fresh perspective moving forward?

_____

_____

_____

_____

Prayer

Father, thank You for opening my eyes and allowing me to see You in the light of Your love for me, not only as Your child but also as a widow. Your word teaches me that You are my defender and protector, and I am eternally grateful. Help me God, to always put things into proper perspective as I continue to move through this process called grief. Amen

Today I am grateful for:

_____
_____
_____
_____

REFLECTIONS FROM THE HEART:

_____
_____
_____
_____
_____

DAY 11
Celebrate Small Victories

Psalms 35:3b NLT
"I will give you victory."

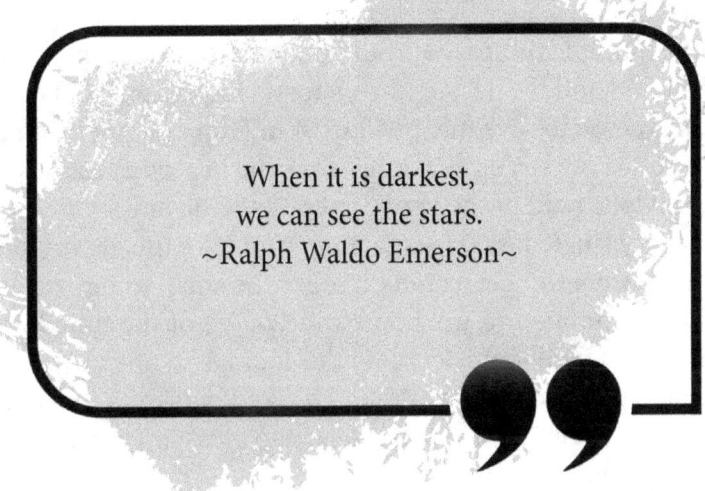

When it is darkest,
we can see the stars.
~Ralph Waldo Emerson~

Each day we need to celebrate every single accomplishment we have achieved, no matter how small it may seem to you. Our greatest mistake is to think that the small things do not matter, but they really do. I read a quote somewhere that says, "Sometimes big things make little difference, and sometimes little things make a big difference." Do not discount small things and believe you are not progressing. In the beginning stages, grief can wipe you out physically, mentally, and spiritually. It can exhaust you beyond anything you could ever imagine. Just to lift your head off the pillow or turn over in the bed could be an exhausting and daunting task.

One of the most challenging moments to accomplish is finding the emotional and physical energy to get out of bed. Life has dumped tragedy into your lap and given you the enormous assignment with the unexplainable challenge to "Survive." Right now, you struggle to believe you are equipped on how to hold on to your sanity and may feel lost. Please know that you can and will survive!

As you read this book and work through the pages, count this moment as a "VICTORY." God tells us, "I will give you Victory." It is crucial during this time to learn how to celebrate small successes. You may not think getting out the bed is a victory, but it is. You may not believe that taking a shower is a victory; it is. Yes, sweeping a floor, washing a dish, fixing a cup of coffee, going to the mailbox are all victories, especially in the early stages of grief. The first day a tear did not drop is a huge "VICTORY!"

The multiple things that could not initially be accomplished have now shifted and we declare it a victory! Isaiah 12:2 NLT says, "See, God has come to save me. I will trust in Him and not be afraid. The Lord God is my strength and my song; he has given me VICTORY." We shall take hold of the very presence of God and know He is with us in every single task. He is saying, "You have the victory because I am Your strength." Let us not discount the small things we do.

I was confined to my home nearly 99% of the time for several months, and finally mustered up the courage to open my front door and stand in the doorway. When I walked outside, I saw that a new season had begun. The flowers started to blossom, and the grass was turning green.

It is vital for widows not to see or run their lives like a marathon. We cannot leap tall buildings with a single bound. We are not Superwoman or Superwidow; do not place yourself or allow anyone else to put you in that position or category. Your success in moving forward is made up of small victories that will lead you into a new season of your life. Honor It. Embrace It. Celebrate It.

1. Can you remember when you did not have the strength to get out of bed?

2. From what you read in this chapter, what was your first victory? Did you celebrate it? Did you feel good about it?

   _____
   _____
   _____
   _____
   _____

3. Are you ready to move into your new season?

4. Write down all your victories, no matter how small.

   _____
   _____
   _____
   _____
   _____

Prayer

Father, each day I awake I know I can celebrate another victory. I celebrate my love for You as You walk with me step by step in this journey. God, Your presence shall continue to overtake me as I walk with You in strength and victory. Holy Spirit, I honor each milestone as a victory as I travel this road with you. Amen

Today I am grateful for:

_____
_____
_____
_____

REFLECTIONS OF THE HEART:

_____
_____
_____
_____
_____

DAY 12
Why Am I So ANGRY?

Psalms 122:7a KJV
"Peace be within thy walls."

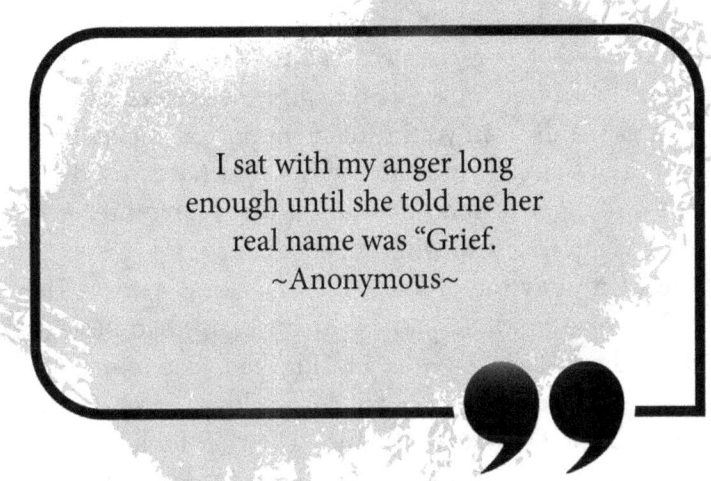

I sat with my anger long enough until she told me her real name was "Grief.
~Anonymous~

How did the life I once had go from meaningful to feeling meaningless?

I would sit in anger at the emptiness I was carrying each day, which left a taste of embitterment within the walls of my soul.

Anger is the one stage of grief that seems to be the hardest to manage because it is so well hidden. At times, it hides behind our smiles and laughter as we proceed with everyday life. Anger can take on many forms. The sole purpose of feeling angry is to "disrupt peace."

Anger gives the illusion that we can move through the shock and denial of our pain. We even try to bargain with the guilt of grief, but we still get stuck on ANGER. The pain from anger may cause us to feel as if we have been cheated in life or that God has let us down. Moments of anger can rise out of nowhere like a WAVE! It can pop into existence when:

1. Something is broken in the house.
2. A bill is past due.
3. Your child needs help with their homework.
4. The car has to be fixed.
5. The lawn needs to be mowed.
6. Preparing for the holidays, birthday parties, anniversaries, or vacations, and the list goes on.

The above list is a constant reminder that there were certain areas your loved one took care of, and now they are no longer here. Those extra hands from your spouse supported you and the needs of the home as a shared responsibility, but they have now departed, and you can no longer depend or lean on them anymore. Anger shows up with a vengeance and will take center stage.

One of my favorite TV shows was Good Times. There was a particular episode where James (the husband) had passed suddenly in an accident, and his wife, Florida had just returned from the funeral. When they arrived home, her children were asking her if she was alright. She said, "Sure, I'm fine." Then she looked at her children with an ease of calmness and a smile, and told them to go to their rooms while repeating that she was okay.

Florida begins to hum a song under her breath as she began to clean the table. Suddenly, she stopped and took a deep breath. Florida proceeds to pick up a dish from the table and threw it as hard as she could on the floor. As the plate shattered into what seemed like hundreds of pieces, she shook both fists in the air and cried out, "Damn…Damn…Damn!" This particular moment resonated with me so much because I could see and feel the anger of her pain. There are times where we really try to keep it together, but sometimes we can no longer hold back the anger (or rage) and just explode.

One day, I just wanted to take a sledgehammer and bust holes in the walls, tear the cabinets down in the kitchen, and break every dish in the house. There was a wave of inner anger that needed to be controlled. After a while, we may begin to feel guilty about our anger, and how it has consumed too much of our existence.

Have you ever become so angry at the anger, and it feels like a never-ending cycle? We need to acknowledge our anger and let it know that it cannot take over who we are, and we cannot allow it to hold us in its decisive grip.

It is necessary to recognize and face your anger because God has given us the power to defeat it. Philippians 4:8 NKJV says, "Finally, brethren, whatever things are true, whatever things are noble, whatever things are just, whatever things are pure, whatever things are lovely, whatever things are of good report, if there is any virtue and if there is anything praiseworthy—meditate on these things." We may be angry, but we need to know that it can be a healthy emotion when dealt with properly, especially dealing within the confines of one of the stages of grief.

We must ensure that our misplaced anger does not spill over onto our children and the people we love. One day, my anger was misdirected at my oldest son. I thank God that he was strong and mature enough to know that it was the anger of his mother speaking to him and not the heart of his mother. When anger is displaced, it can disrupt and/or destroy family, friendships and relationships. We find that hurt and pain can become an A-Bomb (Anger Bomb), vowing to explode and destroy anything in its path.

When we do not address and face anger, others will feel the wrath of our pain and rage. We must recognize the internalized force of our pain. Internalized anger can bring emotional devastation, physical harm to our bodies, and spiritual injury to our souls. We can make a choice today to not allow anger to harden our hearts toward others or God. It is imperative for us to pray and ask God to bring peace within the walls of our heart, spirit, soul, and mind.

1. Search your heart and ask yourself if you are angry with God, and if so, why? Please be honest.

   _____
   _____
   _____

2. Has your anger affected the people around you? If yes, explain how.

   _____
   _____
   _____
   _____

3. Ask yourself, "What can I do to help alleviate the anger within me?"

   _____
   _____
   _____
   _____

Prayer

Father, Your words say that I can be angry, but sin not. God, help me to find peace within the walls of my heart. If there is any hidden anger within me that has not been dealt with, search my heart, oh Lord, so that I do not sin against You. I pray that the spirit of calmness and comfort will overtake the spirit of anger. Purge my heart so I can serve You with gladness and retain a heart of praise. Amen

Today I am grateful for:

_____
_____
_____
_____

REFLECTIONS OF THE HEART:

_____
_____
_____
_____

DAY 13
Beauty of the Brokenhearted

Psalms 34:18 NIV
"The LORD is close to the brokenhearted and saves those who are crushed in spirit."

> As far as I can see, grief will never truly end in this lifetime.
> It may become softer over time, more gentle, and some days will feel sharp.
> But grief will last as long as love does forever.
> ~Lexi Behrndt~

One day, my daughter took me on what we would call a "Destination Mother-Daughter Day Trip." It was about an hour and a half before my curiosity peaked as we crossed state lines. I became more and more curious each additional minute wondering, "Where in the world is she taking me?" When we finally arrived, it was in front of a huge white Victorian-style building with massive columns and impeccable sculptured overlays. As we walked up to the home consisting of 15-foot-wide marble stone steps, I realized that it was a very exquisite Tea House.

The location was discreetly hidden and concealed in a quaint community you might have never known existed. The owner was very friendly in her welcome as she introduced herself, seated us, and placed teacups and matching kettles on the table. I reached for a particular cup due to its unique color and engravings. I don't believe anyone noticed, but my eyes caught a tiny hairline crack extended from the rim to the handle. The minor fracture did not deter or take away from the beauty of this particular dish. I really didn't care about the crack because I simply loved the uniqueness of the cup. It reminded me of the beautiful colors you would admire in fine tapestry.

I sat there and was reminded of our lives as widows. We may be broken and cracked in some places, but still beautiful. The memories of some of our marriages come to mind. The pain of losing our husbands can cause us to feel broken or shattered in many areas of our lives. We must hold onto the beauty of realizing that our brokenness does not negate what has been left behind in our hearts.

If something is destroyed, crushed, or lost, and we did not genuinely love it or place any value on it, that particular item did not impact us one way or the other. On the other hand, when something of "great value" breaks that is priceless and irreplaceable and brings us to a place of broken heartedness, it's only then that we can see and appreciate its beauty. It's the beauty of the brokenness that our grief will bring us to. Kenji Miyazawa once wrote, "We must embrace pain and burn it as fuel for our journey."[4] We can find our beauty despite our pain and brokenness, which can bring us to a special place in Christ Jesus. God comforts the broken-hearted and His light of love continually shines upon us.

In retrospect, I could have asked for a different cup, but I didn't. When I poured the hot water into it, it still stood the test, and the beauty still shone through it as if it was a new cup. Some, if not all, of our marriages may have consisted of some sort of flaws, cracks, and maybe even on the verge of being broken over the years. Yet, none of these things took away from the artistry, love or beauty of our marriage. There is beauty in your brokenness that death nor grief can take away from you. The beauty of God shines in and through you.

1. Do you feel broken at this time during your journey?

2. Has your pain and brokenness fueled you in any way? If yes, how?

   _____
   _____
   _____
   _____

3. List ways your brokenness has opened your eyes to various ways you can use to help and bless others.

   _____
   _____
   _____
   _____

Prayer

Father, I am so broken, but I know You are the Potter, and I am the clay. Fashion me, God, for Your good pleasure. I know my fractured moments did not dim the beauty of Your glory in my life or my relationship with You. Thank You for using me and loving me through my numerous flaws. May my brokenness facilitate others to see the beauty of their brokenness. Amen

Today I am grateful for:

_____
_____
_____
_____

REFLECTIONS OF THE HEART:

_____
_____
_____
_____
_____
_____

DAY 14
What's Next?

Psalms 143:10 NIV
"Teach me to do Your will, for You are my God; may Your good Spirit lead me on level ground."

> If you are struggling today, remember this; you have survived everything you've gone through up to this point. The best day of your life is yet to come. There are still people you haven't met and things you haven't experienced. You can do this.
> ~Unknown~

Now that an essential part of your life has ended with your spouse, what does your next chapter look like? The thought feels a little scary, right? I was thinking about my next chapter while speaking to a wonderful friend of mine. I told her it feels like a page has turned in a book that was written for my life.

Even though we may not know what's in the next chapter, we see a page has turned, and an episode has ended. WOW... such a tragic ending in a core chapter is now complete. The anticipation of a new chapter deepens as we begin to turn our page. Now what? How will this chapter begin? What's going to happen? How will this person survive? Will they make it through? These are the questions we ask ourselves when we are reading a novel, but the novel we are reading is called "YOU." What could we begin to write for our future? What do we foresee down the road? One of the hardest things we will ever have to do is turn a page in a new season without our loved one.

Strength is one of the most courageous tools we will need to pull on as we move forward. Your mind is like a pen in your hand, and you are the canvas in which the future can be written. You have the tenacity, the vision, and insight to begin writing the next chapter of your life.

Although your soul mate is no longer with you on this earth, you still have the power to write the next part of your story. As you cling to the memories and hold onto God's hands, the first sentence we might consider is asking God what is "His" will for our lives. Even if all we have are memories, we must hold onto God and His word. 1Thessalonians 5:18 states, "In situations no matter what the circumstances be, we must be thankful and continually give thanks to God, for this is the will of Our Father for you, in Christ Jesus." I know I have asked this question millions of times. God, what is this thing called "will?" I have come to realize His will is His perfect plan for our lives.

If you could write the next chapter of your life, what would it be? Consider giving your chapter a name and make it personal. Allow it to speak to the inner person God is calling forth. What would you want your story to be about? Don't forget; you are writing the story.

How do you see the next chapter continuing? Is it going back to school, starting a business, retiring, volunteering, or working in ministry? Does your story include mentoring, writing a book, teaching classes, new health goals, spending more time with family, or traveling? The sky is the limit, and this is a perfect time to redefine new milestones.

I wish to encourage those who feel paralyzed in their thoughts right now and cannot begin to consider their next steps in moving forward at this time. The pain is too fresh and totally understandable. I know how numb it feels because I was there. I was unable to maneuver around the pain for what felt like a lifetime. I didn't feel like moving into the next challenges of my life. However, your chapter must still be written.

Reflect on the fact that you have the power to start somewhere and take small steps to push through the pain. Please rest in the assurance that there is a "next" chapter. You are the author, the writer, and orchestrator of how you see the life that God has given you. Allow the strength of the Lord to apply your vision on paper as you are guided to walk out your next season. The word of God tells us in Habakkuk 2:2 NKJV, "Write the vision and make it plain," so I challenge you to start writing!

1. What does the next season look like in your life?
   _____
   _____
   _____

2. Is it too painful to think about what is next in your life?

3. List things you envision for your life.
   _____
   _____
   _____

4. How would you title the next chapter of your life?
   _____
   _____
   _____

Prayer

Father, I come to You in the precious Name of Jesus. You continue to strengthen me, and I look forward to the next chapter in my life. I long to know You in the beauty of Your holiness even more. I rest in the assurance that You have sweetly gathered my husband in Your loving arms, and the picture of Your care for him has helped me to embrace this difficult road. Guide me to write my vision as I see it through Your eyes and what You desire for my life in this next chapter. Amen

Today I am grateful for:

_____
_____
_____
_____

REFLECTIONS OF THE HEART:

_____
_____
_____
_____
_____

DAY 15
When the Tears Just Won't Stop

Psalms 6: 6-7 NLT
"I am worn out from sobbing. All night I flood my bed with weeping, drenching it with my tears. My vision is blurred by grief; my eyes are worn out because of all my enemies."

> I hide my tears when I say your name,
> but the pain in my heart is still the same.
> Although I smile and seem carefree,
> there is no one who misses you more than me.
> ~Unknown~

What can someone really say that would decrease the flow of tears from falling after a tragic loss of a spouse? Nothing! After my husband's death, I had no idea that it was humanly possible for a person to expel the unimaginable number of tears I experienced shedding each and every day. Buckets of tears are no match for rivers of tears. I could not articulate the pain or talk about my loss because it was too draining to discuss.

The pain absorbed way too much energy to verbalize my agony, so I communicated with others through text. My friends, pastors, and family would text me each morning to check on me. One morning, I texted them to share a particular scripture God gave me. I told them I was so exhausted and could not stop crying, no matter how hard I tried. I would wake up in misery and tears. I would go to bed with the crippling afflictions of sorrow, and the tears would begin all over again. Just to breathe caused me pain, yet with each breath I knew I had to take the pain to survive. Each morning I woke up it felt as if someone was sitting on my chest stopping me from taking in the most smallest amount of air.

The numerous boxes of tissues were no match to the tsunami of tears which burst forth within my spirit. Nothing I had could help soak up all the tears that would take up residency and drench my bed day and night.

My heart was unable to fathom or understand the suffering. I could not get a grip on the pain. No matter how hard I tried, it was beyond my knowledge or comprehension.

Psalms 6:7 NIV states, "My eyes grow weak with sorrow; they fail because of all my foes." When I think about the latter part of the verse, I believe it speaks to our strength and how our foes are the "emotional being" we are currently struggling with at the time.

We may become overwhelmed as we battle the foes of disappointments, anxiety, depression, fear, abandonment, confusion, sadness, shock, guilt, numbness, etc. However, we know that nothing lasts forever, and neither will the flow of our tears.

There is a quote that says, "A thousand words can't bring you back, I know because I've tried. And neither would a million tears. I know because I've cried." Is this how you feel at times?

In Revelations 21:4 NIV, the word of God says, "He will wipe every tear from their (our) eyes." I believe when we cry, Jesus takes in our pain. Our tears are precious to the Father, and He keeps them close to His heart. Allow your tears to flow freely to God. He will catch them as He will catch you and not allow you to fall.

1. Can you relate to David in Psalms 6:6? Does it touch on any of the pain you feel/felt during the initial part of your grief? How?

   _____
   _____
   _____

2. In Psalms 6:7, the NIV version states, "My vision is blurred." Has your heartache and tears blurred your vision of God's love? If yes, how do you see God differently?

   _____
   _____
   _____
   _____

Prayer

Father, Your word says that You will wipe away every tear from my eyes. You have seen my pain and have kept track of all my tears and sorrows. You have collected each tear I have shed, placed them in Your bottle, and recorded each one in Your book. God, You continue to provide strength to my frailty each day. Thank you, Father, for holding my tears so close to Your heart. Amen

Today I am grateful for:

_____
_____
_____
_____

REFLECTIONS OF THE HEART:

_____
_____
_____
_____
_____
_____

DAY 16
H.O.P.E.
Hang On; Pain Ends

Psalms 31:24 KJV
"Be of good courage, and He shall strengthen your heart, all ye that hope in the LORD."

> Grief is never something you get over. You don't wake up one morning and say, "I've conquered that; now I'm moving on." It's something that walks beside you every day.
> ~Terri Erwin~

During the various stages of grief, many of us will try to find something positive to dwell on each day. Our thoughts may turn to scripture, a song, a positive quote, motivational speeches, or just words of inspiration. We're looking for anything to help us soothe our wounded soul. One morning, I was reading and came across a particular word, HOPE. The acronym's meaning, "Hang On Pain Ends" was as though something immediately lit up my spirit.

One phrase gave me a whole new vision of hope. There is "hope" in pain, but the pain will eventually end. I knew at that moment, I needed to view HOPE from a new perspective. There will be times that you may feel hopeless, but hang on because the pain does end. When I saw this for the first time, it made me go back to the very first day of my loss.

The feeling of hopelessness, abandonment, and loneliness

engulfed me. My mind would consider the complicated journey of strategically maneuvering through the thicket and maze of feeling hopeless. But God tells us in His word that He is our HOPE. We can't lose hope at this time in our lives because that is one of the primary sources we need to cling to. There is hope we will laugh, smile, and dance again.

We will live again, and YES, we may even love again. We need to have the hope of thriving and not just surviving. It is our hope in Christ Jesus that will bring us to a healthy mindset.

Right now, we probably can't see the forest for the trees. We feel desolate and, in a place, where we think no one is there for us. Our thoughts have possibly shifted to being in a dry desert place. No one may even recognize or understand that your mind is drowning in a sea of confusion and commotions.

Pain is not permanent and does not last a lifetime. You may feel as though you cannot take the hurt one more day. No more tears can be cried, and the heart cannot take the strain… not another day. Psalms 39:7 KJV tells us in part, "My HOPE is in thee" because He is my refuge; therefore, we must have HOPE.

Allow God to soothe, hold, and calm you. Open your heart to Him and allow Him to be Lord in your life. It's OK, and it's going to be OK. Know that the God we serve holds us in the palm of His hands. He is ever-present with us, and Jesus has gone before us. Psalms 146:5 KJV says, "Happy is he that hath the God of Jacob for his help, whose hope is in the LORD his God." God is our HOPE.

1. How do you find yourself placing your hope in God's hand?

   _____

   _____

   _____

2. List some of the areas you are feeling hopeless.

   _____

   _____

   _____

3. List how you will relinquish your hopelessness and replace it with hopefulness.

   _____

   _____

   _____

Prayer

Father, when I begin to feel pain and my heart begins to ache, I know You are Jehovah Rapha, my Healer, and my Hope. Hold me in Your arms and allow Your Spirit to quiet my soul. Thank You, Jesus, for You are the resurrection. When You arose with all power, so did my hope. Continue to go before me with Your spirit of hope, love, and joy. Amen

Today I am grateful for:

_____
_____
_____
_____

REFLECTIONS OF THE HEART:

_____
_____
_____
_____
_____
_____

DAY 17
Grief Does Not Have Me; I Have Grief

Psalms 97:1 CEB
"The Lord rules. Let the earth rejoice. Let all the islands celebrate."

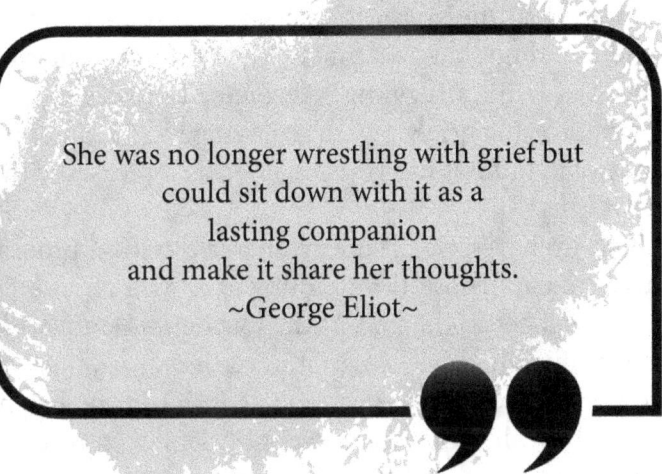

She was no longer wrestling with grief but could sit down with it as a lasting companion and make it share her thoughts.
~George Eliot~

After hibernating for nearly four months, there were times I could barely make it to the bathroom without collapsing on the floor in despair. I woke up one morning (still struggling with all my emotions) and shouted, "Grief, you don't have me, but I have you!" At this time, I knew I was in a battle for my mental, physical and spiritual life. My thought of making this statement alone puts the power back into my hands. Grief was not going to hold me hostage any longer. The pain would eventually bring me enriched knowledge toward my only purpose; face the journey and bring glory to God.

One morning, I gave a brief demonstration to my wonderful widow's group. I had a large bottle of soda (representing us). I shook up the bottle vigorously, which expanded due to its elements (representing all our emotions from grief). Then I shook up the bottle again and passed it around while asking if anyone wanted to open it. Guess what? Nobody did! Everyone declined! They knew that the soda would have spilled on them and everyone in the room, which would have made a complete mess.

The demonstration was an exact illustration of how grief moves in us. I took the bottle and began to open it a tiny bit at a time with just enough minimal air to be released. The representation showed some things can be handle if we consider the pace second by second, and breath by breath. Our emotions can be similar to the shaken soda bottle, which could explode if we do not try to control it.

I knew I had the power to release grief moment by moment, in my time. It did not have a stronghold on me, for I had the authority over it. Was I still struggling? Absolutely! However, I understood that I was carrying grief; it wasn't carrying me. If you have grief, you can control it, but if it has you, it will do as it pleases with you every chance it gets.

When we have grief, it means there's a critical process that will lead us to our purpose through prayer. If you choose to let go of grief, you will get to the part of the journey where it will loosen its grip over your life. I believe grief never leaves us, but it won't have the power to take control over you as it did in the beginning. You will begin to realize that the power of grief lessens every single day as you release it little by little, and start to move forward on your journey. You will wake one day and realize the grief you once had is no longer in the same realm where it once existed.

It is my heartfelt desire to help someone walk out their grief process. There are ten basic ways I offer to you in dealing with grief. These milestones consist of areas I needed to accomplish in my stages of grief, and will be especially helpful to those who are at the "beginning of their initial stages." I highly recommend that you consider taking small steps in the beginning until you are ready to proceed to the next milestone.

For some individuals, you're trying to move from a very dark place of feeling life isn't worth living without your loved one to managing the simplest tasks. You do not have to do all ten things at once.

Consider the accomplishment of one or two tasks each day. You want to do something to help bring yourself back to the normality of your life. Washing a dish or sweeping the floor is an essential initial step. Believe it or not, those tasks were very hard for me at the beginning of my grieving process. I felt as if someone told me to climb Mt. Everest barefooted, or complete the 2-mile Ironman Triathlon Swim (as a non-swimmer)! I guarantee you will feel victorious with one completed task as you regain your power over grief. Please consider the following solutions:

1. Get out of bed, if only to sit alongside it for 5 to 10 minutes. Put your feet on the floor and thank God for another day. It will be an easy task for some; for others it will be a huge challenge, especially if you feel heavy-hearted and low in spirit. Either way, it will be a great accomplishment after completion.
2. Wash your face, even if you do not feel like taking a shower. Look into the mirror and see that you are strong and still standing. Feel the water on your face and try to relax.
3. Brush your teeth, which will allow you to feel a sensation other than the sensation of pain. It may seem elementary to you, but a pure struggle for so many others. I was in bed paralyzed for six weeks, and brushing my teeth was not always on the top of my list.
4. Brush your hair and remember how you once looked. You are focused on accomplishing "one" thing right now. Remind yourself that you are still a beautiful woman despite what you are going through. Pamper yourself by getting your hair done. Enjoy a pedicure, manicure or massage.
5. Find any scripture you desire and read it. Here are two if you do not have the strength to search for one:

    Psalms 68:5 ESV, "Father of the fatherless and protector of widows is God in His holy habitation."

    Psalms 34:18 NIV, "The LORD is close to the brokenhearted and saves those who are crushed in spirit."

    Grief MUST be put into its proper place. Grief is not your enemy; it's a process that needs to be compartmentalized. It is a part of you that has attached itself to your heart, which is still connected to the love for your husband.
6. Play worship music. Worship music soothes your spirit and

soul. Remember how David's played music to soothe Saul's soul? Allow worship music and the Holy Spirit to minister to you during this time (whatever healthy type of music you choose is also an option).
7. Open the door to your home or open a window and stand there for a few minutes as you inhale and exhale fresh air. Exercising this task will remind you that you're still alive. The freshness of the wind and the sun upon your face will feel like God is embracing you.
8. Write an "I Can" statement to yourself. It doesn't matter what you write. Just make it one positive thing. "I can get out of bed," "I can fix my breakfast," "I can go to the park," or "I can walk a mile." You are stronger than you think.
9. Sit and meditate on one thing you are grateful for. Gratefulness brings a spirit of peace to you, and an appreciation of what you still have left on this earth. "I'm grateful I made it through the night," "I'm grateful for the memories," and "I'm grateful for my family." Gratefulness can bring healing to your spirit and soul. Your spirit and soul will thank you.
10. Light a lavender candle. Lavender is known as a healing scent and helps with anxiety, insomnia, depression, and restlessness.

Hold yourself and cry if you want. No one can hug or hold you like God because only the two of you know exactly what you are going through. Hold yourself and allow God to embrace you. It's OK to cry as long and as hard as needed. God sent his Holy Spirit to comfort you, so allow Him to be your Comforter.

Additionally, I am a great advocate of getting counseling. If you need counseling or medication, I strongly recommend seeking a professional or certified assistance. Your support can include a doctor, counselor or spiritual advisor. They are also there for you during your time of need.

Identify the professional doctor, counselor or spiritual advisor you will call if you find that you need assistance. Write down their names and numbers for immediate access. Put their numbers in your phone for a quick reference.

1. What are some of the things you can do when grief arrives?
   _____
   _____
   _____

2. Identify one of the basic tasks you will do this week.
   _____
   _____
   _____

3. Describe one step you will consider reclaiming power over grief.
   _____
   _____
   _____

Prayer

Father, thank You for always being there for me. Your word says that You are the ruler over all things. Your word also says we have power in our speech. Father, I speak life and strength during this time of my journey. I shall set a guard over my mouth of speaking anything other than healing to my soul. You have given me authority over grief. Thank You, Lord, for bringing me joy in my sorrow and light for a dark path. Amen

Today I am grateful for:

_____
_____
_____
_____

REFLECTION OF THE HEART:

_____
_____
_____
_____
_____
_____

DAY 18
God Wired Me That Way

Psalms: 139:14-15 NLT

"Thank you for making me so wonderfully complex! Your workmanship is marvelous—how well I know it. You watched me as I was being formed in utter seclusion; as I was woven together in the dark of the womb."

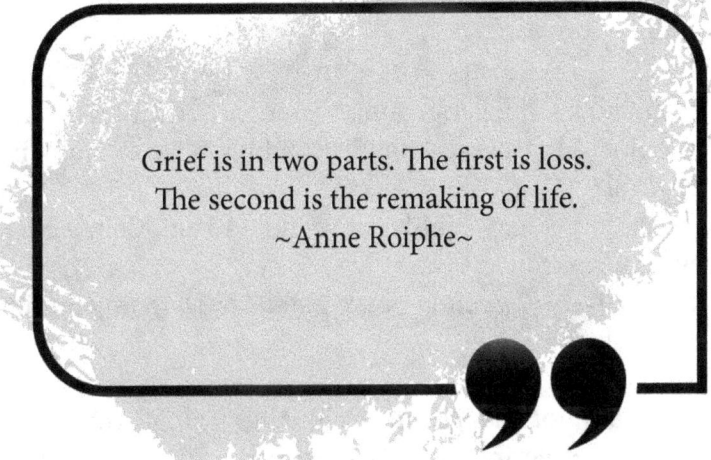

Grief is in two parts. The first is loss. The second is the remaking of life.
~Anne Roiphe~

After my husband transitioned, I could not understand why it took me so long to get out of bed. I did not want to interact with people. Yet, I observed other ladies who lost their husbands were able to proceed with a "normal" life. They enjoyed being around people, and life seemed to move on for them. Some ladies took the bull by the horn and commanded their lives to forge ahead. Yet, I found myself struggling, and aimlessly wandering around.

I would beg God to help me figure out why I can't get myself together. Why do I long for the seclusion and security of my room? Why can't I bear to see anyone's face or hear another voice trying to console the inconsolable? Then, as I sat in a conference, I heard God speak one day and say, "You are not wired that way." Each of us has our own personality and character which some may call personality traits. I studied personality traits many years ago and discovered that we grieve according to our various personalities.

My personality is a part of who I am, as yours is a part of who you are. Each one of us has our own personality traits. I would recommend that you take a personality test, which can help you understand how you may not only deal with grief but how you deal with life in general.

The Personality Profile information is based on a comprehensive personality plan by Maria and Florence Littauer. The test consists of four personality traits, which are Melancholy, Sanguine, Choleric, and Phlegmatic. The characteristics of each personality are provided below:

1. Melancholy - The Perfectionist - sincere, sensitive and analytical.
2. Sanguine - Extrovert - popular, bubbly, love talking and seeks approval.
3. Choleric - Leader - highly active, not too emotional and needs a sense of control.
4. Phlegmatic - Peaceful - easy-going, hide their emotions and extremely low key.[5]

Grief does not change our personality trait; it works within the confines of how we are wired. Grief does not stop who we were born to be. The word of God tells us that "He formed us, He is the Potter and we are the clay." The Lord gave each of us our own individuality, and how we handle our grief process does not need to be compared to others. God wired each of us differently, but our commonality is the love and longing for our husbands. Grief is horrific for everyone.

Embrace your uniqueness of grieving; trust the workmanship of God's heart and hands to allow you to grieve and comfort you through the process.

1. Do you recognize how you are grieving in comparison to your personality trait?

2. What personality traits are you, Melancholy, Sanguine, Choleric or Phlegmatic?

3. How has your grief affected your personality trait?
   _____
   _____
   _____

4. Can you identify and embrace how your personality or character is "wired?"

Prayer

Father, You formed me with the complexity of Your hands. You created me and shaped me specifically for Your purpose. Please do not let me wander away from the person You taught me to be and show me how to celebrate my uniqueness in You. Lord, help me embrace who I am, where I am, and where You take me on this journey. Amen

Today I am grateful for:

_____
_____
_____
_____

REFLECTIONS OF THE HEART:

_____
_____
_____
_____

DAY 19
Hidden Pain

Psalms 43:3 KJV
"O send out thy light and thy truth: let them lead me; let them bring me unto thy holy hill and to thy tabernacles."

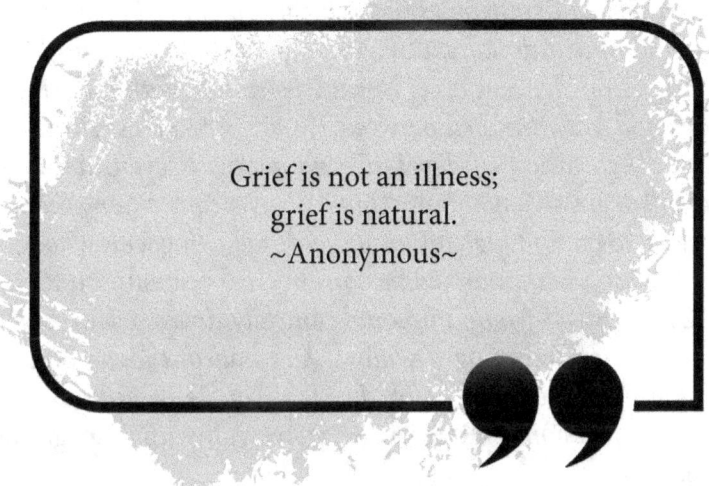

Grief is not an illness;
grief is natural.
~Anonymous~

Helpless **I**solation **D**esolation **D**epression **E**mptiness **N**umbness

There are times where widows find themselves often in denial. I walked through the denial of what happened, my loss, and yes, even in the denial of my pain. As a widow, we may even struggle to accept that we are depressed and want to escape this part of our life. The denial becomes our "HIDDEN" pain. We feel we must be strong, invincible, and full of strength. Widows dare not talk too much about our feelings for fear of sounding like a broken record, repetitive and needy.

The concoction of reliving how much you hurt mixed with missing your loved one can be enormous. Therefore, we begin to hide our feelings as much as we can. We mask the agony of the pain that overwhelms us and knocks on the door of our hearts during those long, lonely nights. We are alone with our thoughts and memories and find ourselves in a state of weakness. We are deprived of physical, mental, and spiritual strength to keep going. Some of us, knowingly or unknowingly, become DEPRESSED!

Depression is not a contagious disease or dirty word, and it is definitely not a sign of weakness or even a choice, as some may think. The following information was in the Oxford Journals cited by PubMed Central (PMC), which stated:

"Widowhood is associated with a multitude of adverse physical and mental health outcomes including psychological distress, physician visits and institutionalization, and higher rates of morbidity and mortality. Prevalence rates of clinical depression within the first year of widowhood are estimated between 15% to 30% across studies, though subclinical elevation in depressive symptoms is even more common. Although depressive symptoms diminish over time among the widowed, they seem to remain high for many years following widowhood, at least in comparison with married persons in cross-sectional studies."[6]

"One-third of women become clinically depressed within the first few months of becoming a widow. And half of those women had to continue their medication for the next couple of years due to their clinical depression." (Reference: www.widowmight.org/emotions/depression)

The bible gives an example of those who were depressed or had anxiety due to a particular situation. We can look at David who was troubled, or Elijah who was discouraged, weary and afraid. Jonah was angry and just wanted to run away from it all, and Job lost his wife and family and wanted to die. Even Jesus was in despair for the journey He had to endure for us at Calvary. Any of these words resonate with your grief? Have you experienced the emotions of feeling troubled, discouraged, afraid, lost, or angry? How many emotions are you experiencing?

There is a quote that says, "Grief is like living two lives. One is where you pretend that everything is alright, and the other is where your heart silently screams in pain." Sisters, we may hide our pain from others, but we can never hide our pain from God, and He doesn't want us to.

Psalms 145:14-16 ESV states, "The LORD upholds all who

are falling and raises up all who are bowed down. The eyes of all look to You, and You give them their food in due season. You open Your hand; You satisfy the desire of every living thing. The Lord is righteous in all His ways and kind in all His works". Psalms 107:28-29 NIV says, "Then they cried out to the Lord in their trouble, and He brought them out of their distress. He stilled the storm to a whisper; the waves of the sea were hushed."

My God, when we hit those WAVES (and we will as part of our healing process), suddenly you may find yourself bursting into tears in the middle of a sentence, a shopping trip, in the car, or cooking dinner. God says in His word that He will hush the waves. He will calm the WAVES for us when they hit. Please be mindful that you WILL experience waves in the grieving stages. "Grief is like the ocean; it comes in waves ebbing and flowing. Sometimes the water is calm, and sometimes it is overwhelming. All we can do is learn to swim." ~Vicki Harrison[7] We will learn to swim through the grief we experience, and we will become phenomenal swimmers through every wave of grief we encounter.

One of the greatest assurances is knowing that we never have to hide our feelings from the Lord. God is all-knowing, and He is always there to hear us. Hebrews 4:13 NIV states, "Nothing in all creation is hidden from God's sight."

Our Helplessness, Isolation, Desolation, Depression, Emptiness, or Numbness is not "HIDDEN" from God because He cares for us, and His eyes are on us. He will strengthen and cradle us, speak to our mind, and listen to us. His love is never hidden from our hearts.

1. What are some of the feelings you have hidden or denied yourself?
   _____
   _____
   _____

2. Have you been honest and truthful with God regarding your feelings?

3. Write a letter to God about your pain. He is your Father; tell him the truth about the suffering of your loss.

Prayer

Father, I ask that You hear my heart of truth today. Although You are all-knowing and nothing is hidden from You, I have hidden in my heart things I haven't spoken to You regarding my loss and pain. Hear my prayer, Lord, as I empty and release every detail I've hidden in my heart, soul, and spirit unto You today. Amen

Today I am grateful for:

_____
_____
_____
_____

REFLECTIONS OF THE HEART:

_____
_____
_____
_____
_____
_____

DAY 20
Don't Give Up!

Psalms 118:13 NASB
"You pushed me violently so that I was falling, But the LORD helped me."

> The reality is that you will grieve forever. You will not get over' the loss of a loved one; you will learn to live with it. You will heal, and you will rebuild yourself around the loss you have suffered. You will be whole again, but you will never be the same.
> Nor should you be the same, nor would you want to.
> ~Elizabeth Kubler-Ross~

You may feel as though there are times where life has pushed you into giving up. Failing and falling are two destructive actions that try to control your thoughts, but God will show up and snatch their very existence every time if we "Don't Give Up." Allow me to share something that caught my eye. I was watching a cartoon one day, and a miner was digging for diamonds. He continued to dig relentlessly for days while sweating and feeling achy. After several days of digging and exploring with no success, the miner "gave up" and left.

Shortly afterward, the next miner came along and began to dig in the exact same place where the other miner grew weary and frustrated, and within a matter of minutes, he hit an ore of diamonds! If only the first miner held on and kept digging a few minutes longer, he would have received his diamonds (his breakthrough). We cannot miss our breakthrough, so "Don't Give Up!"

A description of the hole in your heart cannot begin to describe your true feelings right now. A widow's mind may experience a sequence of thoughts. Your whole world may have felt like it has fallen apart. Some are struggling to live past the pain. Don't give up! You're fighting against the reality of feeling empty and dead inside. In the beginning, there is a void that seems too empty to be filled.

Your life is riding a merry-go-round of sorrow, but there is nothing merry about the sorrow you are feeling. There may even be an inner torment beyond your imagination that you are struggling with this very moment. The pain from walking a fine line in your thoughts is so intense, you feel there is no one you can talk to. You STILL cannot give up! Keep your focus on God and allow Him to fight for your sanity! You can do all things through Christ who strengthens you.

You may be sitting in a counseling office and thinking, "They know the textbook concepts, science, theories, and social aspect of my grieving, but they do not understand the depths of my pain." The pain has become like free radicals running rapidly through your body. The confusion in your mind is so conflicting that the reward for having fallen so deeply in love with your husband now feels like punishment and agony. We dare not speak about these feelings to others, but they are too raw, authentic, and real to dismiss.

I am here to let you know once again that It's OK not to be OK, but it's not OK to bypass getting the help you need. Studies and Research have shown that widows reported experiencing more depression after the initial year following their loss.

According to information in the U.S. Library of Medicine School of Psychology, one of their studies showed that Widows with husbands who were ill are more depressed during the illness. Depression after their death was less because those widows were already in the grieving process prior to the death of their loved one. Depression creases during the initial year of widowhood, and remains elevated well after the first year.[8]

If you are in a place of desolation, darkness, abandonment, don't give up; seek the help you need. Anger, anguish and frustration can promote a sense that the whole world is caving in on you, but do not quit this fight. Don't Give Up.

You are not voiceless, powerless, or silent, and your emotions are justified! Hang in there for another minute, another hour, and wake up for another day to feel the sunlight upon your face. Although you may think the entire weight of the world is on your shoulders, please understand that there is help for you. Don't Give Up.

If you must check yourself into a hospital or call someone to sit with you throughout the day or night, press your way through the thought of inconveniencing someone and ask for assistance. You can do it, but please, don't you DARE GIVE UP!

1. Have you ever felt like giving up and not wanting to go on?

2. Do you feel you need professional or medical help?

3. List things in your life that is not worth losing.

   _____
   _____
   _____

4. Who would benefit from you not giving up?

   _____
   _____
   _____

5. What is the reward of life that will keep you moving in the right direction?

   _____
   _____
   _____

Prayer

Father, Your word says in John 14:27 NIV, "Peace I leave with you; my peace I give you; I do not give to you as the world gives. Do not let your hearts be troubled and do not be afraid." God, I trust and hold onto Your words and find solace and comfort in Your love and peace. For today I will not give up on myself, and I will never give up on You. God, I will give up all my pain to You because I trust that You can handle my pain far more than I can. Amen

Today I am grateful for:

_____
_____
_____
_____

REFLECTIONS FROM MY HEART:

_____
_____
_____
_____
_____
_____

DAY 21
Lead Me in Your Path

Psalms 32:8 KJV
"I will instruct thee and teach thee in the way which thou shalt go; I will guide thee with mine eye."

> But grief is a walk alone,
> others can be there and listen. But you will
> walk alone down your own path,
> at your own pace, with your sheared-off pain,
> your raw wounds, your denial, anger and bitter loss.
> You'll come to your own peace, hopefully...
> but it will be your own, in your own time.
> ~Cathy Lamb~

As a little girl, I would snuggle very close to my grandmother in church. I loved to feel the warmth of her body as she would rock back and forth with the rhythm of the hymns. She would sing the melody to the songs as the organist played on an old, brown wooden, tattered upright piano. I felt so much joy just to look upon her face and hold her soft hands.

My grandma would close her eyes and sway her head back and forth. Her melodic, soprano voice was music to my ears and brought me so much comfort for I will always cherish the songs that came from my grandma. I can recall her singing one particular song:

"Lead me, guide me, along the way. Lord, if you lead me, I shall not astray. Lord, let me walk each day with thee. Lead me, oh Lord, Lead me."

In the quiet times of my day, this song would resonate and deeply fill my soul. It would pull on my heartstrings and speak to where I was in my life journey.

When I think about this specific song, I am reminded of our journey as widows. It would be so advantageous to ask God to "lead us and guide us" along a grievous path we must now travel.

We never desire to explore such a painful journey and would give anything to wish our current passageway of life without our spouse never existed. I know, I often asked God, "Is this the only road to my purpose?" If so, it doesn't feel good at all, and maybe I don't want to reach my purpose if the devastation is so costly. Do you think this way at times? Guess what? It's OK to feel that way, and no need to think otherwise for the moment. It would be so easy for us to become lost and stray off course if God was not leading and guiding us. We must take time with God every day and pray to Him to lead and guide us to where He wants us to be.

There are times we can be overwhelmed and feel submerged and overtaken in our emotions. Moses must have felt the same way during his own experiences. God led Moses out of Egypt, across the Red Sea and into the wilderness. God will guide us through our waves and experience with grief. We always learn from our experience because pain is never wasted, even if it benefits someone else in the future.

One of the byproducts of pain is experience and knowledge. We will never forget what we have learned on our journey, and with our experience, we will be able to help someone else on their grief walk. We praise God that our purpose in life is not attached or dictated by death, but through the blood of Jesus Christ.

Just as Moses.... you may not know initially how or if you are going to make it to the other side of your journey, but guess what? God knows and has a master plan for your life. He is going to lead and guide you to the other side of grief. I offer to share a few words to express to God throughout your day:

- Lord, let me walk with You today.
- Lord, hear my prayer this day.
- Lord, hold my hand each day.
- Lord, give me the vision for my life today.
- Lord, hold me close to You daily.
- Lord, give me the strength right at this moment.
- Lord, lead me, oh Lord, lead me every single day.

1. How are you allowing God to lead you during this time on your journey?

   _____
   _____
   _____

2. Name a wilderness experience during a moment of grief.

   _____
   _____
   _____

3. Find a scripture(s) that speaks of God leading someone through a trying time, and meditate on it today. Allow His words to encourage you this week.

   _____
   _____
   _____

Prayer

Father, each day I live, I seek Your face. I need You to lead me to where I need to be in You. I entrust You with my life, and I know You will not lead me astray. Lord, I know Your hand and love will guide me to where You have called me to be for this season. Allow my experience on this journey to minister and bless someone else. Amen

Today I am grateful for:

_____
_____
_____
_____

REFLECTIONS FROM MY HEART:

_____
_____
_____
_____
_____

DAY 22
Guilt or Regret

Psalms 18:6 NIV
"In my distress, I called to the LORD; I cried to my God for help. From his temple, He heard my voice; my cry came before Him, into His ears."

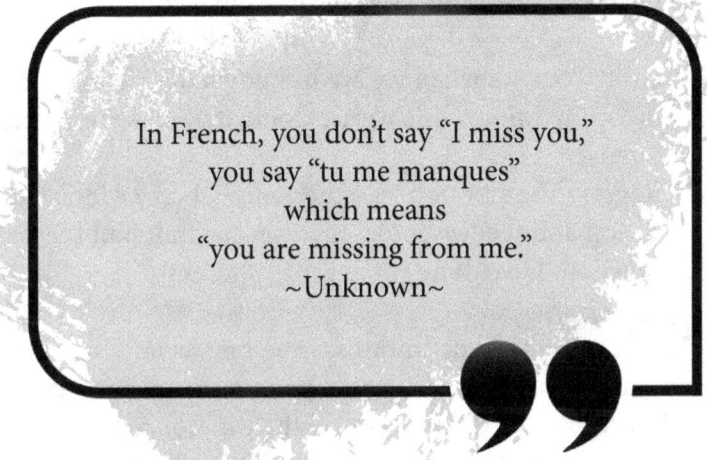

In French, you don't say "I miss you,"
you say "tu me manques"
which means
"you are missing from me."
~Unknown~

One of the statements I've heard from every widow I've ever met is, "I wish," followed by "The Guilt or Regret." Let us look at a few "I wish" comments.

I wish I had seen the signs.
I wish I listened to God.
I wish I were there more for my husband.
I wish we had not postponed that special date night.
I wish we had not postponed our vacation.
I wish we never had that argument.
I wish we had moved.
I wish we spent more time together.
I wish I told him to go to the doctor.

I wish I told him to stop working so hard.
I wish I helped him take better care of himself.

I wish, I wish, I wish. Can you relate to any of the wish comments above? Are there any "I wish" questions you are thinking of right now that is causing you to feel guilty or regretful? I think guilt and regret are interchangeable and ambiguous at times. I wanted to look up the meaning of the word Guilt (one of the primary clinical five steps of grieving) and Regret.

According to Merriam-Webster Dictionary:

- Guilt - occurs when we are in knowledge of and consciously in wrongdoing while we are doing it, or a commitment of an offense.
- Regret - the emotion we experience when we look back on an action and feel we could, may, or may not had the control or power to have done something differently.[9]

When I view both definitions, I see one as an emotion and the other as an action. My goal is not to go into the mechanics of guilt or regret, but to ensure we understand the difference between the two words. As you read the definitions, which category do you feel you are dealing with right now? Whether it's guilt or regret, the word of God tells us in Psalms 38:4 NIV, "My guilt has overwhelmed me like a burden too heavy to bear."

It is normal to have guilt or regret for a loved one who has passed. When someone dies, we begin to think we should have visited, called, or made some form of connection with the person. We must realize that life will happen, and we cannot walk in the guilt or condemnation of their death.

Romans 8:1 NIV states, "Therefore, there is now no condemnation for those who are in Christ Jesus." If God can forgive us, then we need to forgive ourselves. After my husband passed, I struggled with regret. I regret that if I had not slept in so late, I might have encouraged him to hold off working in the heat that day.

I've worn myself out by constantly asking, "What would've happened if I gave him something to do around the house?" Maybe it could have deterred him from being in the sun. Could my request have saved his life? Oh, the guilt! Oh, the regret!

I have met many widows with various stories along my journey. Some of them expressed their love, adoration, and marital bliss memories of their spouses, and others speak about the pain, betrayal, hurt, and disappointments they were experiencing. My personal story, along with the stories of the widows I've connected with, compelled me to add this chapter regarding guilt and regret. We must ensure we can relate to the importance of both types of pain.

How do you deal with the grief of guilt, regret, unforgiveness and unsolved issues you may have experienced with your loved one? You can no longer physically talk to him, look him in the eye, and express your deepest feelings to him. What happens now in your life, especially for recent widows who suddenly lost their husbands without warning?

One of the best things we can do is forgive ourselves for any wrongful thinking. Why is this significant? For starters, let's revisit the "I Wish" list at the beginning of this section. If you did not see the signs, forgive yourself for that. If you believe you did not listen to God, forgive yourself. You wished you helped your husband take better care of himself; forgive yourself. If you had a difficult argument with your spouse before he passed… that's a big one, and forgiving yourself is crucial. Consider walking through the list and ask for forgiveness. Once God has forgiven us, we must now forgive ourselves. Psalms 103:12 KJV states, "As far as the east is from the west, so far hath he removed our transgressions from us." Forgiveness is one of God's greatest gifts to us.

It is essential we remove guilt and regret from within our spirit, regardless of who was right or wrong. You do not want to carry anything in your heart that would hinder your mental, spiritual, or physical healing. One suggestion to consider for healing and moving forward is to write a letter to your husband. List everything you need to release, including any guilt or regret. Additionally, you can write a love letter to your spouse and express all the loving words you have longed to share with him.

Put your heart on the tip of your pen and allow your inner

emotions and thoughts to flood the page. Pray that God will allow you to speak from your heart as needed. Once you've completed writing your letter, burn the paper and allow the ashes to be taken away by the waves of the ocean, the winds of the sky, or wherever you choose to release it.

Guilt or regret will attempt to resurface, but do not allow it to take up residence within your heart or spirit. Writing your letter to your spouse should be a moment that will free you. Grant yourself the opportunity to have the emotional release you need to walk in the freedom and liberation God intended for your life.

1. Do you have regrets or feel guilty? If so, ask yourself why.

   _____
   _____
   _____

2. Do you feel you need to forgive yourself or your spouse? Why?

   _____
   _____
   _____

3. Do you have unforgiveness in your marriage?

   _____
   _____
   _____

4. Are you allowing yourself to walk in "true" forgiveness?

5. If you write a love letter, what would it say?

Prayer

Father, help me to empty myself to You completely and release any regret, guilt, or unforgiveness I have held in my heart. Free my spirit from any condemnation I am carrying within my soul. God, I open myself to Your word that says You have removed all of my transgressions, hurt, and unforgiveness. Amen

Today I am grateful for:

_____
_____
_____
_____

REFLECTIONS FROM MY HEART:

_____
_____
_____
_____
_____
_____

DAY 23
Lean Into the Pain...
Lean Into the Grief

Psalms 62:1-2 NLT
"I wait quietly before God, for my victory comes from Him. He alone is my rock and my salvation, my fortress where I will never be shaken."

> Some of us have been through things so traumatic that the human mind isn't built to handle it, but we fight and persevere every single day and night. If that's not strength, I don't know what is. You are a survivor.
> ~Unknown~

When you first read the topic of this section, it may not make any sense at all and sounds like an oxymoron. Why in the world would someone lean into pain, or even think about leaning into grief? As a matter of fact, wouldn't you rather run as far away as you can from pain and grief? One thing of certainty is that you cannot run from God, from the pain of grief, or the grief of having pain. It is impossible to run from any of these truths.

At the writing of this book, I am 10 months into my husband's transition. My mind refused to rest, and nights are very restless, leading to the battle of constant insomnia. One particular night (or should I say morning), I looked at the clock which read 2:43 am. Obviously, I could not sleep, so I decided to go to the local 7-11 for some coffee. I returned home and just sat in my car as if I was frozen in time. Losing every sense of the essence of who I was, I found myself drifting into a place where I felt I no longer existed. Suddenly, the "WAVE" manifested, and tears began to stream down my face as I thought of my husband.

My heart soaked in a permanent stain of sorrow, which had taken up residency and became a part of my everyday life. The tears filled my eyes and began to trickle through my shirt onto my skin. I immediately felt the same familiar ache the day the police officer informed me that my husband had passed. All I could do was begin to scream and beat the steering wheel. I wailed from the very depth of my soul. I remembered thinking, who is screaming like this? Where is this sound coming from? When will it stop? I felt I had an outer body experience.

All I was thinking was how could God had done this to me, how could he had disappointed me like that? I temporarily lost who I was and almost who God was to me. I continued to scream and cry for what seemed like hours. Right at this moment, I realized that something had lifted from my inner soul. A sense of relief and release occurred, and I began to feel a small amount of healing take place. It seemed as though God engulfed me in the warmth of His arms and covered me with the robe of His peace. In spite of my anger and disappointment towards Him….He embraced me with His love.

As you begin to shift toward progression, your many attempts to embrace the journey may make you feel you have been dealt an unfair hand. The process of moving through your pain still requires you to move forward. Grief will not allow you to bypass it without first embracing it. Initially, you may try to replace it with things to do. As widows, we will look for ways to find substitutes to offset the pain. We will shop, drink alcohol, binge eat, party, take pills to numb the pain, do drugs, go from place to place, and some may prematurely jump into a new relationship.

We will do anything to divert our pain. Other people will share words suggesting that "You should try to keep busy," "You need to get out more," "Maybe it's time you do something different," "You need to move on," "You will find someone else," "You are young, you have a lot of life left," and the list goes on and on. Does any of these suggestions sound familiar to you? I would get so angry when people would say or insinuate that I should move on. Some people just don't know what to say.

The reason they are offering these suggestions could be because they have become uncomfortable with your pain and the uneasiness of properly responding to your grieving process. Allow me to add that they being uncomfortable is not "your" problem. When other people make comments you struggle to accept, these responses may indirectly push you into a place you're not ready to embrace at the moment. You are not allowed the necessary time to lean into your reality and your true feelings. The end result for some is finding a substitution for the pain you are experiencing instead of leaning into it and allowing it to heal you.

Second Timothy 1:7 KJV says, "For God hath not given us the spirit of fear; but of power, and of love, and of a sound mind." There are times we become fearful of what grief can do to us. I know this because I was so afraid of the mental, spiritual, and physical damage grief was causing. I felt I was out of control and could no longer identify with myself. Who was this person I was becoming? But the word of God tells us He has:

1. Not given us the Spirit of Fear,
2. He has given us Power,
3. He has given us Love,
4. He has given us a Sound Mind.

The four certainties mentioned above provide us with the strength to lean into our pain and grief without fear, but with power, love, and a sound mind. It is imperative to find God's words on strength during this time and use His scriptures with prayers as reinforcement for your heart and mind.

I was secluded and isolated for so long during my grieving period that my loved ones were worried about my mental and physical health.

I knew their concerns were genuine and very appreciative, but I was unable to articulate what I was walking through and could not communicate my feelings with anyone. The best thing I could do at the moment was to write a letter and send it out to my family and inner circle of friends. Giving them the assurance that I needed time and time with the Father and Him alone.

1. Do you feel people are trying to rush you through your grief?

2. What are some of the things you have done in trying to ignore or run from grief?

   _____
   _____
   _____

3. What experience do you have (if any) of people trying to warp speed your grief?

   _____
   _____
   _____

4. How did you react, and what would you say to them after reading this section?

   _____
   _____
   _____

5. Do you feel you are genuinely facing grief?

6. Do you feel you need to write a letter to those closest to you?

Prayer

Father, You are my strength, and I know You are with me as I lean into grief and learn from it. I pray over all areas of my life while I'm working through this process with You. God, You have given me the spirit of love, power and a sound mind. Lord, I do not have room for anyone else on this road with You. Thank You Father, for Your graciousness towards me as we journey on this road together. Amen

Today I am grateful for:

_____
_____
_____
_____

REFLECTIONS OF MY HEART:

_____
_____
_____
_____
_____

DAY 24
R.E.S.T
Restoring, Empowering, Strengthening, Thriving

Psalms 37:7a NKJV
"Rest in the LORD, and wait patiently for Him."

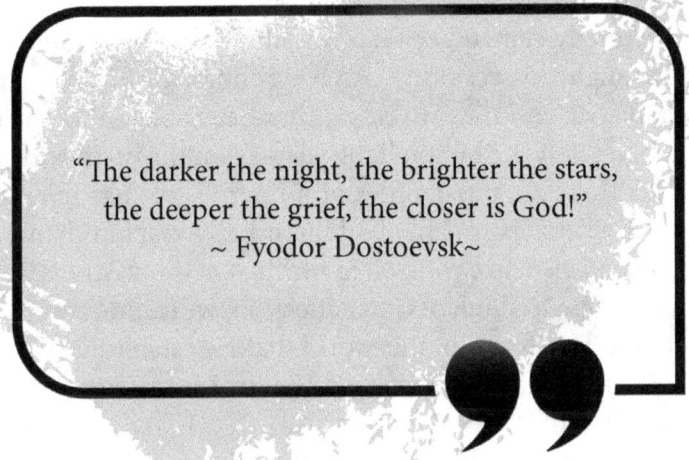

"The darker the night, the brighter the stars, the deeper the grief, the closer is God!"
~ Fyodor Dostoevsk~

One of the most important things we need to do during our time of grief is to REST. REST is a place of stillness and quiet time to be strengthened and to simply breathe. I believe we can relate to both of these needs. Regained strength requires replenishment and fuel for our mind and body. Equally, there are times where a simple breath or to fully exhale is all we want to do during this time in our lives. We may feel like death is smothering us, and we are vigorously fighting a battle to breathe. However, we must come to that place of totally putting our trust in God and "REST" in him.

When the perpetrators of fear, anger, and bitterness fill our mental reservoir, they will challenge our ability to rest. It is imperative we keep our eyes on God and know that He will always comfort us. Grief will not have more power than God's love and affection. There will be challenges ahead to find rest (due to various obstacles), but we must hold onto our spiritual vision and know that God is there.

Psalms 9:10 KJV states, "And they that know thy Name will put their trust in Thee: for thou, LORD, hast not forsaken them that seek Thee." As we walk through our grieving process, we need to diligently seek a place where we can lay our head, rest, and trust our Father will be right there with us. When I think of God in all of His sovereignty, omnipotence, holiness and glory, I know He cares so much for us that He desires us to rest in Him. Psalms 8:4 NKJV says, "What is man that You are mindful of him, and the son of man that You visit him?"

I distinctly remember God revealing how important we are to Him through this scripture. As we ponder, God is the Creator of heaven, earth, and the universe. It has been stated that the universe is approximately 3.5 billion light-years from the earth with 2 trillion galaxies. There are possibilities of numerous planets in each galaxy, and the universe is roughly 93 billion light-years in diameter. Now envision and visualize yourself in the mist of this vastness. Wow!! So, when we begin to think of God's affection, we cannot comprehend or fathom His love for us in this world that He established. The Creator of "ALL" things deeply expresses His love from heart to heart and breath to breath.

Our Father gave life to everything above, yet the bible says He rested on the seventh day. Rest must be significant if God took a whole day to do it and spoke about it specifically in His word. As we go about our day, whether we're having a fabulous one or full of grief, we must take time to rest. The Lord is mindful of us and cares for us.

Psalms 91:1 NKJV states, "He who dwells in the secret place of the Most High shall abide under the shadow of the Almighty." As we abide under the shadow (protection and shelter) of God and seek His sanctuary, He is there to protect and lead our lives. Numbers 6:25 reminds us that the Lord makes His face shine upon us. Can you imagine the face of our Holy God shining upon you right now? Matthew 11:28 KJV says, "Come unto me, all ye that labor and are heavy laden, and I will give you rest." Look at the beauty of God's love; He knows precisely what we need.

Grief has become like a weight within our spirit, and we have labored with it as a mother giving birth for the first time. The labor came with unsuspected pain, like something we have never felt before. It was incredibly difficult as we struggle to function between the pain.

How many times have we become tired, weak, and weary and said, "If only I can just find a place of rest"? I still remember all the sleepless nights I spent alone after my husband passed. God desires for you to come and lay your head upon His shoulders, present your burdens at His feet, and allow Him to guide you through your journey of grief to a place of rest. What an awesome God! We must always remember that one of the best ways to find rest is to commune with God daily. Let's choose to soak in His presence for a crucial time of rest and peace.

1. Do you feel you are truly resting in God according to Psalms 91:1?

2. What are some of the things you need to lay at the feet of God so you can rest?

   _____
   _____
   _____

3. Identify the circumstances or people who have hindered your rest?

   _____
   _____
   _____

4. What can you do to obtain rest?

   _____
   _____
   _____

Prayer

Father, teach me to rest in You and lay all my burdens at Your feet. Help me to continue to commune with You and to be still. Allow me to rest in the knowledge of Your power, sovereignty, and love. Knowing that Your word says You are mindful of me is assurance that I am always in Your thoughts.
Thank You, God, for thinking about me.
Restore me, Lord,
Empower me with peace;
Strengthen and deepen me with Your word so I can
Thrive in a purposeful life of Your entrusted love.
Amen

Today I am grateful for:

_____
_____
_____

REFLECTIONS OF MY HEART:

_____
_____
_____
_____
_____

DAY 25
Healing in Stillness

Psalms 46:10a KJV
"Be still, and know that I am God."

> My scars are a testament to the love and the relationship I had for and with that person. And if the scar is deep, so was the love.
> ~Unknown~

When I was a little girl, I noticed that my father walked with a limp. I asked my mother, "Mom, why does daddy walk like that?" My mother told me the story (from his mother) of how my dad climbed a tree, fell, and broke his leg when he was a little boy. Although his leg was properly set, he did not follow the instructions of the doctor. My dad was supposed to be still to avoid weight on his leg, and when he chose not to follow the doctor's orders, it did not heal properly. I thought that could not be true, so I went to my auntie, my dad's sister. I asked her why my dad had a limp, and she told me the same story.

My father was aware of the circumstances but would not be still long enough to heal. The leg eventually regained functionality, but not the way it should have, leaving him with a noticeable limp. The timing to transition to a full healing process was incomplete.

Time can heal a wounded soul. As widows, we can feel so broken that we miss the opportunity to be revived. When we decrease the necessary time to heal, it will eventually become noticeable in our lives. When we derail our moment to heal, we could end up experiencing an internal and spiritual limp. There are critical adjustments that are carved out for our healing process to occur. We must allow God's hands to make the necessary repairs within us.

God wants us in a place of stillness to reset and restore what needs to be applied to our lives so we can come into a place of healing. One of the biggest mistakes we can make as widows is to allow other people to place a false belief in our healing process. God's desire is not for someone to bully us into a timeframe that tries to supersede when and how we move outside His timing. We do not want to be guided by the healing opinion of others; God's opinion is plenty. Our grief journey and healing process belong to Him. Therefore, we must take time to quiet our soul and spirit to receive direction from the Lord.

Only God can tell us how long it will take us to move forward. Jeremiah 1:5 KJV states, "Before I formed thee in the belly, I knew thee." He knew us before we were in our mother's womb; He formed us and knows everything about us. God knows how deep our wound is, where the fractures are located, what He needs to do, and exactly where to apply the healing salve. For some individuals, moving forward may take a few months or years, but you will never go wrong with receiving your instructions and timing from God.

As widows, moving too quickly may hinder our healing process and cause us to make irrational decisions. It is imperative to appoint a trusted advisor to assist us with decisions concerning pre and post-funeral business matters and legal affairs. We must also ensure God's timing remains center stage when considering a possible relationship to replace the lonely space in our lives. Our safest healing tool is stillness is God, especially in this area.

As I revisit my story regarding my father's younger years, he decided not to listen to his parents and went right back outside to climb the trees again, which only compounded the fracture. Years later, I believe he realized his limp would never go away due to his healing process decisions. Although he never complained, I know it hindered his ability to move freely, and regretted not taking the time to heal correctly.

My dad had the ability and flexibility to walk, but I never saw him run. If we want to move forward in the manner God desires, we cannot cripple our mental, emotional and spiritual mobility. The Lord has essential information and critical instructions He wants to download to us. Psalms 46:10 KJV says, "Be still and know that He is God," and Exodus 15:26 KJV states, "For He is the God that healeth us." God understands, realizes, appreciates, and comprehends our lives.

Listen to the Lord and move with Him. Rest and be still in the presence of our Father. When we are still, we hear God more clearly in our quiet place. It is so important that we sit and wait "with" Him because far too often we are waiting "for" Him. All we truly need is His presence.

Everyone heals differently. Some of us will always carry the scar of an injury for a lifetime, while others will not. We can make a vow right now to refuse our imperfections to prevent us from making progress in the years ahead. We will not limp in our decisions, nor will our scars hijack the healing process. My sister, please be still in the Lord and listen to Him. Take time in prayer to hear Him, so he can apply the Balm of Gilead upon your soul and bring you to a place of healing during your time of stillness.

1. Are you being still in God? If not, what is causing the hesitation?
   _____
   _____
   _____

2. Are you fearful of being still?

3. How much time can you allow/commit yourself to have with your Father daily?
   _____
   _____
   _____

4. Write down what God is saying to you each day during your moments of stillness with Him.
   _____
   _____
   _____

Prayer

Father, help me not to move too quickly in my healing process. Guide me to move only as You direct so I can completely heal with the assistance of Your love. Your word tells me to be still in You and become more intimate with You. Speak to my heart, oh Lord, as I sit with You. My ears are opened, and I listen intently to Your voice to hear every word. It is pure joy to sit still in the radiance of Your presence. Amen

Today I am grateful for:

_____
_____
_____
_____

REFLECTIONS OF MY HEART:

_____
_____
_____
_____
_____

DAY 26
His Hands; His Heart

Psalms 89: 28 & 34 NKJV

"28: My mercy I will keep for him forever, And My covenant shall stand firm with him."
"34: My covenant I will not break, Nor alter the word that has gone out of My lips."

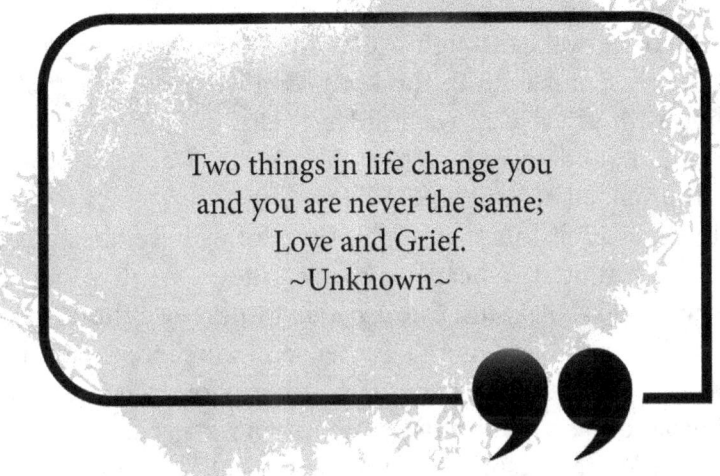

> Two things in life change you and you are never the same;
> Love and Grief.
> ~Unknown~

There is a saying when you cannot see God moving, then trace where He has been. When we cannot see God's hand moving or think His hand has not protected us, then we must trace God's heart in our lives. Isaiah 49:16 NIV says, "See, I have engraved you on the palms of My hands; your walls are ever before Me." He holds us close to Him, and we must trust God's heart and depend on His word. Isaiah 55:11 KJV states, "So shall My word that goeth forth out of my mouth, it shall not return unto me void." We need to trace and reflect on the last time God showed up. He is the same God then as He is right now.

One of the main comforting thoughts is "Remembering" when God showed up for us in our time of grief. During our most difficult moments, there may be times you believe God has taken His hands off of you, or He has allowed punishment to consume your life and thoughts. You may even consider a bold move and question God on His decision. "God, where was Your hand in this?" "Lord, why didn't you heal?" "Why didn't you protect my husband?" Prayerfully, we will realize that God's loving heart is massive, and He's always there for us and with us. We must press into knowing His heart, and His presence, no matter what.

We must never lose sight of knowing that Jesus can handle our pain and our sorrows. God does not take pleasure in our pain or our suffering. He is not a covenant breaker; God is a keeper of His covenant with us.

When we walk through a life-altering moment, it will require us to increase our faith in the Lord. Can we trust Him 100% while dealing with grief? Can we still have faith in Him while in denial, shock, guilt, and regret? What? You mean, we need to believe in Him through all of our pain? YES we do!

In times of feeling distraught, some of us have questioned God for the first time! I've heard so many widows say that they did not question God, but I sure did. I needed to know "The Why" of my husband's death. God is my Father, and I believe I can ask Him anything. I will never question His authority or decisions, but losing my husband was beyond a tragedy. I may never get an answer, and I'll be satisfied with a response or non-response.

God has given us the indelible grace and mercy of His love, which cannot be not revoked, erased or altered; it is permanent and forever. God's heart aches when your heart aches. His word tells us in Psalms 56:8 NLT that He keeps track of all my sorrows. Can we be honest? How many of the following comments have we expressed?

- God, where were You that You did not stop "Death?"
- For the first time, my faith has been shaken to the core.
- I felt God abandoned me.
- I feel so alone.
- I felt like God turned his back on me.
- I thought about walking away from the church and God.
- I don't know what I believe anymore.
- I was/am angry with God.

My hope is to drop a seed of encouragement today. You may not see God's hands on one of your greatest tests, but that doesn't mean His heart is not towards you. Psalms 91:11 KJV states, that we are so dear to God's heart that he has given us angels to guard and protect us because we are that precious to Him. You may not feel Him or see Him, but He will never leave you.

The eyes of the Lord are on the sparrow, and we know He is watching over us. God knows every step we take at all times and what we are going through.

1. Do you feel God has abandoned you after the loss of your husband?

2. Do you trust the heart of God toward your situation?

3. Have you questioned God in the passing of your husband?

4. What were your questions to Him?
   _____
   _____
   _____

5. Do you believe He has given you an answer?

6. Can you trace God in your life? (List the times He did show up for you)
   _____
   _____
   _____
   _____
   _____

Prayer

Father, I know You're the one and only wise God. Even when I cannot feel Your hands, I know Your love surrounds me, and You are always looking out for me. I must trust in all I know of You and always remember that Your lovingkindness is forever present. Lord, I receive Your heart and care for me today and forevermore with an everlasting love. Amen

Today I am grateful for:

_____
_____
_____
_____

REFLECTIONS OF MY HEART:

_____
_____
_____
_____
_____
_____

DAY 27
Never Can Say Goodbye

Psalms 34b:10 NIV
"Those who seek the LORD lack no good thing."

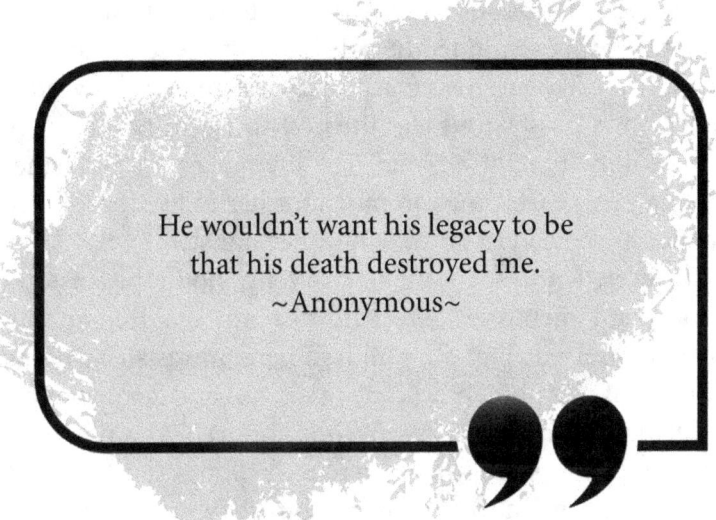

He wouldn't want his legacy to be that his death destroyed me.
~Anonymous~

In this chapter, it may appear as though we are referring to never saying goodbye to our husbands, however, there is a different take on this. The Motown industry released a hit song in the 1970s entitled "Never can say Goodbye" by a soul/pop group called "The Jackson 5." I thought of that song title as I was trying to make a decision to get rid of my husband's possessions, which I believe most widows dread and struggle to do.

My heart and mind went into withdrawals whenever I pondered on letting go of his things. I asked myself, "How can I say goodbye to so many items that reminded me of him?" How can I part from his favorite black checkered suit he was so fond of?" Every time he put it on, I would just smile and ask him, "Are you wearing that suit again?" After the funeral arrangements and paperwork legalities were finalized, I needed to begin the exhausting task of going through his possessions. Can I share that this was one of "THE" hardest things to do on my widow list?

There comes a time whereas widows must deal with the very delicate, and daunting task of the "Big" departure, also known as getting rid of our loved one's things. Again, no two people never grieves the same. Everyone deals with this task differently, which can make the decision very complicated. There was a friend of mine whose husband passed. As soon as he died, she got rid of everything he owned except this one special hat. She told me it was too painful to see anything that reminded her of him. My friend loved him dearly, and they were like two peas in a pod. However, she knew letting go of her husband's possessions was the best thing for her to do. Another friend of mine bought a home. The memories in the former home tugged on her heartstring too much for her to live there without her husband, so she had to move to another house.

However, I did not want to leave my home because there are just too many memories here with him, my children and family. I birthed and raised all of our children here. It was also a home for all their pets. At one point our home was a zoo and farm wrapped up in one during the earlier years with our children. You named it and it walked on all fours or slithered across the floors. Our home included the additional memories of every birthday, graduation, cookout, planted trees, cracks and messages written in the concrete, which are still here. Our entire family memories are vividly alive in our home.

I was at a crossroad and asking myself, "How can you hand over the things that were such a part of him to others? How can you emotionally release the last bit of items, which are physical signs of his existence?"

I looked at all his clothes, vehicles, shoes, lawn equipment, jewelry, etc. Relinquishing these items is like saying goodbye all over again. Some people may feel as though the death of their spouse is reoccurring all over again as they begin to let go of each item. In some instances, the decision to remove the items can feel like you are betraying your husband, and guilt tries to consume you. You may even ask yourself, "Is it too soon?" "Should I or shouldn't I?"

The best decision you can make at this stage is to take one step at a time and work at your own pace... that's the key! There is no rush unless you are under a time restraint and need to relocate to another location. If you are moving, you can secure a storage unit for your loved one's items until you are ready. Of course, you can always keep a few of his possessions for yourself. Remember the chapter on "Letting Go but Hold Onto the Memories?"

However, if you do not have any time restrictions, take your time, and walk at the pace that works for you. Let go of one item at a time. I still remember eight months after my husband's passing, I went into his drawer to grab one of his t-shirts to wear. As soon as I opened his dresser and touched his shirts, I broke down and cried. The initial period may be hard at first but take your time. There is NO RUSH, and remember, you are still grieving.

As you begin to relinquish his items, you may want to give some of them to people who were close to you and your love. Sentimentally, I gave my daughter special cards that she gave to her dad over the years. My son took his wallet with his ID and unique items in it, along with his cell phone, and his number, so he can have his father's voice mail with him at all times. I knew those things would be very precious to them. After the passing of my son's Godfather, his Godmother gave him his Godfather's neckties. He was a pastor, and whenever my son went to church or attended a special event, it meant so much for him to wear them.

Whenever you are ready to move forward, you may want to give your spouse's clothing to relatives, veterans, homeless shelters, or somewhere you know they will be put to good use. The clothes or items of your loved one will bless and benefit someone else. Great memories can occur when your donations are a blessing to others. Imagine one of your loved ones' suits helping someone secure a job after wearing it to an interview. Maybe the nice pair of shoes you provided will keep someone's feet warm. It could be the first time someone's even owned a great pair of shoes. When you begin to look at how the items left behind could be a blessing to others, it will make things a tad easier to "Say Goodbye."

1. Do you feel you are ready to relinquish any of your husband's possessions?

2. Make a list of when and what you are planning to donate in your own time.

   _____
   _____
   _____

3. Name one thing you will be giving away. Set a date when you are comfortable and ready to handle the task.

   _____
   _____
   _____

Prayer

Father, I am so grateful for all You have given me, including the time I had with my husband. So, teach me to let go of material things while holding on to the fond and loving memories that will last forever. I will not allow our time or possessions to become distractions or idols, but I will cherish the loving memories we shared and were blessed to experience together with one another. Amen

Today I am grateful for:

_____
_____
_____
_____

REFLECTIONS OF MY HEART:

_____
_____
_____
_____
_____

DAY 28
SELF-CARE

Psalms 139:14 NASB
"I will give thanks to You, for I am fearfully and wonderfully made; Wonderful are Your works, And my soul knows it very well."

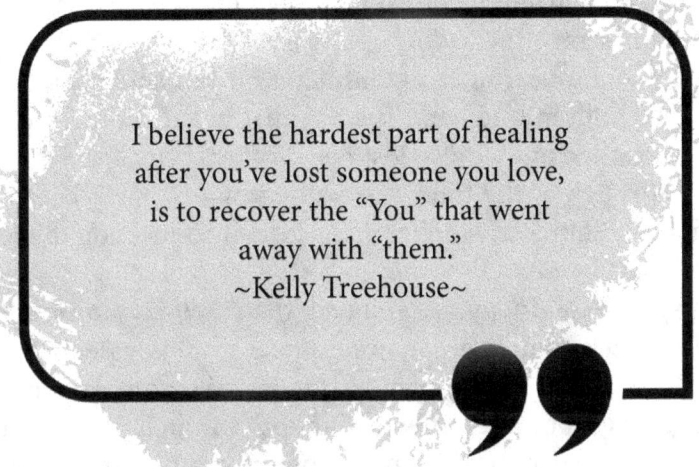

> I believe the hardest part of healing after you've lost someone you love, is to recover the "You" that went away with "them."
> ~Kelly Treehouse~

Self-care is another component that is essential to the grieving process. Many things can compound and complicate our grief, causing us to opt-out of caring for ourselves. During your grieving process, it is crucial to take time out for yourself. Let us review the chapter on REST. Rest and self-care are first cousins in the spectrum of life. It is time we need to be alone with ourselves and with God. We need to take care of ourselves and allow God to minister to us as we practice mindfulness.

During the high point of my grieving period, my health plummeted to an all-time low and my hair fell out. I lost 20 pounds in the first month and gained over 80 pounds in 2 years. I've been in the hospital, had suicidal thoughts, and was on various medications to fight depression, stress, anxiety, and paranoia. My business began to decline, and my body developed numerous medical complications, including lots of aches and pains. I had insomnia, developed broken heart syndrome, and became asthmatic. I frequently experienced panic attacks, mental meltdowns, and the widow's brain fog was no joke. I totally stopped caring about me because I felt there was no "me" without "him."

My mind was spiraling into an abyss of darkness, and I felt there was no returning from this place. The self-esteem I had was running on fumes. My self-awareness vanished, self-motivation was absent, self-care deteriorated, and self-reliance was nil. My self-perseverance was at zero, and anything that identified me as "Self" had just left or died within me. The saddest part of all was when my sister came to me about a year after my husband's death, and shared with me that my children told her, "The day that our dad died, we not only lost our father, but we also lost our mother." Of all the things I was going through at the time, this pained me the most because I had completely shutdown and mentally lost all connection to the person I once was.

Psychology Today once stated that *"Self-care means knowing who you are and knowing your limits."*[10] It is essential to know how to decompress throughout the day. We must take better care of ourselves because we are fighting through a traumatic and devastating experience. Some widows remain in the initial stage of grief and shock longer than others.

Our body, mind, and soul need us to heal from the complexity of our suffering; therefore, it is essential for us to place ourselves first. Jesus said in Matthew 11:28-30 MSG, "Are you tired? Worn out? Burned out on religion? Come to me. Get away with me and you'll recover your life. I'll show you how to take a real rest. Walk with me and work with me—watch how I do it. Learn the unforced rhythms of grace. I won't lay anything heavy or ill-fitting on you. Keep company with me and you'll learn to live freely and lightly." Is Jesus talking to you? Think about it; may the "Unforced Rhythms of God's grace" speak to your heart.

The word of God also tells us in 3 John 1:2 NKJV, "Beloved, I pray that you may prosper in all things and be in health, just as your soul prospers." Some versions read that above all things, He wants us to prosper and be in good health. Notice how God speaks of prosperity and health in the same context. We must realize that our health is our wealth. As widows, it is hard for us to take care of ourselves, especially if we have other obligations. Our schedules can be inundated with responsibilities, including caring for children, jobs, dealing with financial constraints and challenges, mental and medical struggles, and moving into our new normal. This cocktail mixture of emotions is one that leads us to feel utterly overwhelmed. Yet we find that out of all the responsibilities of caring for ourselves we must realize that if we have children, they are our priority. We all know the proper protocol of being on an airplane in case of an emergency, they always say put the oxygen mask on yourself first then your child. We must get help if we are going to help our children. It is imperative to make sure your children get counseling to help them through their grieving process as well, because they need you to lean on.

The first month in the first year is the most challenging time to implement self-care. I know this because it took nearly two years for me to wake up and notice I have not been taking care of myself. The lack of self-care was also a part of Widows Fog. We MUST care for ourselves physically, socially, spiritually, emotionally, and psychologically. We need to set appointments in our schedule to pamper ourselves.

Focus your needs toward physical and mental wellness check-ups. I am an advocate for mental health wellness and all of its components.

Grieving is very hard for many of us. Some may feel the need to stay in bed and sleep all day just to survive from day-to-day pain. Life will move forward; and we must continue because life goes on. Life needs us to fulfill our purpose here on earth.

You will hear me say this often because I really need you to grab hold of this in your spirit, "Death took our husbands but "Not Our Purpose!" Establish a health checklist for yourselves with "Self-Care" guidance. Your list should include proper sleep, healthy nutrition and water intake, exercising, and meditation on the word. Other activities you can consider are joining a gym, scheduling time to go for a walk, joining a widow's group, or a book club. Look into volunteering and listen to positive podcasts and motivational YouTube segments.

I used to hear people say, "It's not about you," but that is a falsehood. During your grieving period, "IT'S ALL ABOUT YOU" and your survival! Engage in activities that make you feel good as you focus on establishing a new normal. Never forget that your body is the temple of God. Allow the Lord to heal your body as you practice self-care.

Write down your feeling and keep a gratitude journal. On each page of this book, you can put daily thoughts of gratitude to reflect upon as needed. After 30 days have passed, revisit your responses and how much you have progressed.

Ladies, this is work. It is going to take work and a heightened level of effort for us to get through this, but the first step in anything is getting the courage and strength to make the initial step. I am confident you will conquer your journey with diligence and determination. Take care of yourself and remember that you have been fearfully and wonderfully made by the very hands of God.

1. Do you feel you have lacked in self-care during your grieving period?

2. What will be your first step toward self-care?

   _____
   _____
   _____

3. List a few areas that have fallen to the ground regarding self-care that you will put in place again.

   _____
   _____
   _____

4. What does the scripture 3 John 1:2 NKJV mean to you personally? "Beloved, I pray that you may prosper in all things and be in health, just as your soul prospers."

   _____
   _____
   _____

Prayer

Father, as I sit before You now, reveal unto me the instructions of self-care for my life. Show me how I can better take care of myself spiritually, physically, and mentally. Thank You, Lord for being the gentle Creator of my rugged vessel, and smoothing the rough places in my life. I forever praise You, oh God, for loving me and teaching me to take care of my temple. Amen

Today I am grateful for:

_____
_____
_____
_____
_____

REFLECTIONS OF MY HEART:

_____
_____
_____
_____
_____

DAY 29
You Shall Live and Not Die

Psalms 118:17 NKJV
"I shall not die, but live, and declare the works of the LORD."

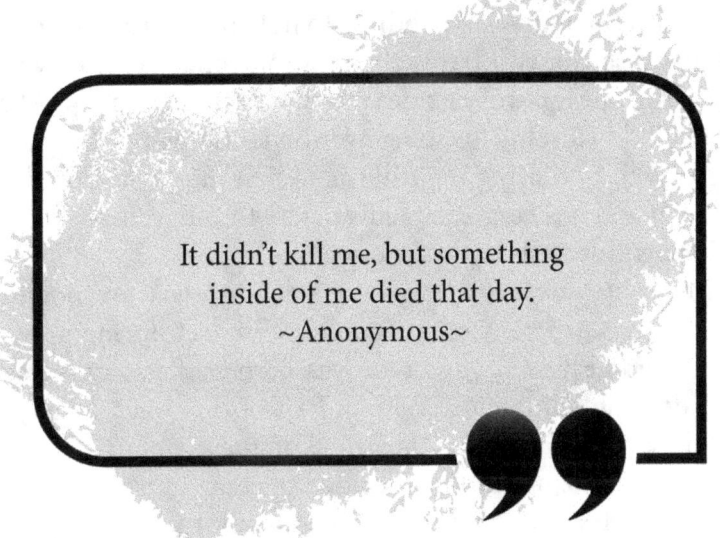

It didn't kill me, but something inside of me died that day.
~Anonymous~

The day my husband transitioned to heaven was the day I felt like I died, and I thought I was in hell on earth. Of all the chapters in this book, this one is so near and dear to my heart. I had to come to terms with the transparency of my journey, so others will not feel as though they are alone.

As widows, we suffer on the day of our husband's transition. It is the very day many of us feel or felt devastation so gut-wrenching, that surely something inside of us must have also died with our spouse. One day, I asked a few questions to my sisterhood widow's group:

1. Do you view death differently?
2. Have you ever wanted death to come for you?
3. Do you feel you are in a place to embrace death more now than before?

Now, allow me to clarify these questions. There is a difference in embracing death if it's your designated time, verses your choice to assist or aid it. I am not talking about someone who is seriously contemplating the act of suicide. If any of these thoughts are being considered, please seek help "IMMEDIATELY!" The reason I am tackling this topic is to speak directly to the heart of those who feel they have nothing to live for and have thoughts of suicide.

I have heard so many stories of other widows committing suicide because they felt they had nothing to hold onto. Please HOLD ON (I did) because you WILL make it, and someone may need your story to survive. The topic of suicide (which is such a taboo topic) has been "off-limits" to discuss for so many individuals. I need to speak to the person who is viewing their life as useless after your loved one has departed and has contemplated suicide. In full transparency, I need to share with you that you are not alone.

My heart's desire is to assure you that you are not the only one that has experienced a troubling mindset during grief. When my Raymond passed, my brain was drenched and immersed with unrecognizable thoughts. Why did I feel this way? I was not able to compartmentalize the intrusion of these unfamiliar thoughts. Every traumatizing emotion decided to come into alliance with one another to destroy and taunt my very soul. I felt damaged beyond repair and became so dismantled.

I felt gravely wounded from within; my very spirit and soul seem to have died and deserted me in the twinkling of an eye. I was psychologically battered, bruised, broken and beaten, and thought it was pure "hell!" Psalms 86:13 KJV states, "For great is thy mercy toward me; thou hast delivered my soul from the lowest hell." God tells me if I make my bed in hell, He would be there. Gravitating to His word is the very lifeline that brought me through my darkest moments. God was there, even in my own private hell.

Please know that there is light at the end of the tunnel, the tunnel is only temporary, and you've got to hold on! The Word tells us in John 10:10 KJV that Jesus said, "I am come that they might have life, and that they might have it more abundantly."

II Corinthians 4:6 ESV says, "Let light shine out of darkness." Wow! These are powerful words expressed here! God's light is about to outshine your darkness!

One day I was sitting and reflecting on the days, weeks and years which had passed. I was thinking, oh my God, I had waited for almost two years to realize I had not died in this process. I literally thought grief was going to kill me. Every part of my being wanted to be with my husband at that time. How could my mind be affected by this type of mentality? Yet, this is the thought pattern of so many women who must now move forward in life without their husbands. I had placed my entire life on hold for over two years! Can you imagine the repeated thoughts that attempted to take place during those years?

I reasoned in my mind that I really shouldn't do anything to move forward. I was going to die anyway due to the enormous stress in my life and on my heart. Hopelessness, depression, and anxiety were singing like a three-part harmony in my thoughts. I felt I became "unhinged" and was sure I would die from a broken heart. I think about what would have happened if I embraced the process, but I couldn't.

I would ask myself, why should I dream, plan or do anything purposeful? In my mind, I kept looking for death and waiting to hear the door knock. Mentally, I imagined peeping out the window, seeking death, wondering where it was, and even hoping it would hurry and show up.

One morning, I woke up and said, "Sherry, you are not dead!" Before I knew it, these words became so clear, "I Shall Live and Not Die!" It struck a chord so deep within my very soul.

Tears streamed down my cheeks as I realized how long I waited at the train station for the death train to pick me up. How would I get on the train if I did not have a ticket or a legal right to board? I was revived with a massive dose of reality... I've wasted so much time, but I know God will redeem my time.

Death happens, and your loss may have taken an enormous part of you, but it did not take "all" of you. In the previous chapter, I talked about the fact that death may have taken your husband but not your purpose or God's glory out of your life. God has given us life, and we must go on living it. Our lives and mindset must shift now to continue to do the work destiny assigned to us.

Sisterhood, let's position ourselves to be present where we are needed, touch the souls that thirst for our love, continue with our dreams and visions, write or modify our bucket list, and do all the things we need to accomplish. Let's commit to dance, laugh, smile, and hope again! We are "Fierce Women of God," and we are a force to be reckoned with…That is US!

One of the disservices I've done to God and injustice to myself was that I literally stopped living my life. I repeatedly share that it is crucial that we must grieve in our own way and time. However, we cannot embrace death if it is not the time to embrace us; until then, we will continue to LIVE, LOVE, LAUGH, and EMBRACE OUR JOURNEY! Take a good look at your Boarding Pass to the destination of Continue Living! I think you're sitting in the seat that says, "PURPOSE!"

1. Since your husband's passing, do you think about death more in relation to your own life?

2. How did you view death after losing your husband?
   _____
   _____
   _____

3. What is one thing you will do to help you shift from thinking about death to living life?
   _____
   _____
   _____

4. What are some of the things you stopped doing in anticipation of death?
   _____
   _____
   _____

PLEASE SEEK COUNSELING IF YOU EVER THINK ABOUT SUICIDE.

National Suicide Hotline 1.800.273.TALK
A 24/7 Line for Assistance 1.800.273.8255
or/Contact your local Mental Health Agency

Prayer

Father, forgive me for allowing the shadow of death to supersede that of the beauty of life and the light You have given me. Help me, Father to breathe again. Allow Your Son to continue to shine upon me and drive away the darkness as I begin to embrace the essence of the life You have so graciously and abundantly provided. Amen

Today I am grateful for:

_____
_____
_____
_____

REFLECTIONS OF MY HEART:

_____
_____
_____
_____
_____

DAY 30
A Stranger in a Strange Land

Psalms 136:16 KJV
"To Him which led His people through the wilderness, for His mercy endureth forever."

> Grief, I've learned, is really just love.
> It's all the love you want to give but cannot.
> All of the unspent love
> gathers in the corners of your eyes, the lump in
> your throat, and the hollow part of your chest.
> Grief, is just love with no place to go.
> ~Jamie Anderson~

Baby Boomers would remember an 80's TV Show called "Quantum Leap." The show's premise was about a former scientist, Sam Beckett (played by Scott Bakula), who through an experiment gone array would find himself trapped in someone else's body. He was frequently tossed back and forth through time due to an experiment that went very wrong. Each week I would watch him to find out which body he was trapped in. Every morning he would wake up, look in the mirror, and find himself in a new era as a totally different person, one who he did not recognize.

Grief can be parallel to the show. You can be at one place in life, and suddenly, death jolts you into a "Quantum Leap Experience." You wake up and wonder, "How in the world did I get here?" You feel you are an entirely different person trapped in a body that's not even yours, along with being in a different place and time. You find yourself trying to adjust to your surroundings, but you're in an unknown place. You have never traveled this road before, and you're on a journey in a foreign land with an unfamiliar body.

The moment takes me back to the time I was confined to my bed for weeks while battling depression and anxiety. One morning, I decided to walk down my hallway and caught a glimpse of a person in the hall mirror. I took a few steps back and stared in the mirror for what seemed to be forever. I kept looking at this unfamiliar person and barely recognized her staring back at me. Who is this strange person? I could see the darkness and sadness of her spirit, and there was no light in her soul. Her eyes had become dull, lifeless, and full of sorrow. All I could hear was my inner thoughts and kept asking, "Who is this stranger?"

I had no concept of who, when, what, why or any type of logical reasoning as to where I was at this time in my life. However, now I can fully comprehend exactly where I was. I had leaped into "The Land of Grief," and the person who was staring at me was a person who had lost a part of her soul. She was only seeing a part of who she was, which was so unrecognizable without her other half. Yes, it was me on the other side of the mirror.

We may find ourselves feeling like strangers in a foreign land, or dodging the path grief is trying to take us. Whatever curve is thrown our way, we must realize that Jesus is not only Immanuel over our lives, but He is also Immanuel over our grief. He is "God (that is) with us" over our grief. He has always been there and will forever be with us every step of the way.

1. Find a mirror and take a good look at yourself. Who do you see looking back at you?

   _____
   _____
   _____

2. What do you want this person to look like?

   _____
   _____
   _____

3. Has grief ever changed your perspective of how you view yourself?

4. Have you ever felt trapped by grief?

5. Have you ever asked yourself, "I do not know the person I am now?"

6. How has grief changed you Mentally? Spiritually? Physically?

Prayer

Father, I come to You in the name of Jesus. I'm unable to comprehend where I am right now. I feel like I am a stranger in a foreign land and lost in a dry and barren place. The place I'm in right now is so unfamiliar to me, but I know You will never leave me or forsake me. Your grace and mercy follow me. Lord, I know You will sustain me in this place and bring Your living water to me in the wilderness. I trust You, God, and I know You are with me always. Help me to feel Your presence as I continue on this road toward healing.

Today I am grateful for:

_____
_____
_____
_____

REFLECTIONS OF MY HEART:

_____
_____
_____
_____
_____

Bibliography/ Source

- Rick Warren-Daily
- Hope with Rick: Best Expressions of Love is Time: October 12, 2016
- Recorded by Danny Gokey: My Best Days-Released March 2, 2010, Written by Lari White, Chuck Cannon and Vicky McGehee-RCA/Nashville
- Burial Planning.com: https://www.burialplanning.com/blog/15-unique-ideas-for-honoring-the-memory-of-a-loved-one
- Quotes by Kenji Miyazawa-www.goodreads.com
- Quotes by Kenji Miyazawa-www.goodreads.com Wired that way-The Personality Profile: Maria Littauer and Florence Littauer: May 2006-Baker Publishing Groups
- Wired that way-The Personality Profile: Maria Littauer and Florence Littauer: May 2006-Baker Publishing Groups
- Widowhood and Depression: New Light on Gender Differences, Selection, and Psychological Adjustment: published online June 28, 2013: https://www.ncbi.nlm.nih.gov/pmc/articles/PMC3894126/: Isaac Sasson and Debra J. Umberson
- Karen Salmansohn-notsalmon.com, Vicki Harrison: 21 Absolutely Heart wrenching Quotes on Loss and Grief
- The impact of widowhood on depression: findings from a prospective survey/https://pubmed.ncbi.nlm.nih.gov/10576303/K B Carnelley 1, C B Wortman, R C Kessler: PMID: 10576303: NIH-National Library of Medicine: National Center for Biotechnology information
- Merriam-Webster All-In-One Dictionary & Thesaurus: Second Edition: 12/2013: Federal Street Press
- Psychology Today-Self Care101: Maria Baratta, Ph.D. LCSW, May 27, 2018: article-Skinny Revisited
- Bible References: King James Version, New International Version, English Standard Version, New American Standard Bible, Common English Bible, New Living Translation, Contemporary English Version. Easy English Bible, New King James Version
- Roget's II The New Thesaurus
- Quotes: Greetingcardpoet.com, Sayinggoodbye.org, Lessonslearnedinlife.com

About the Author

Sherry Medley is a pastor, teacher, facilitator, Retreat and Conference Coordinator. She is the founder of In His Hands Women Ministry, Grace for the Journey Sisterhood for Widows and CEO of a nonprofit, Hand of Hope, Inc. She has a passionate heart for God and a ministry to empower, inspire and encourage women. It is her desire to help others to be healed, set free through the word of God and finding their purpose to bring Glory to the Kingdom of God. As a widow she wants women to realize their purpose and vision was not buried with their husband, but in spite of their situation, there is still purpose within them to be fulfilled for the Glory of God. The inspiration to write this book came from her deep love and loss of her husband. She has been blessed to be a mother of 4 children with 4 grandchildren and 4 great grandchildren.

Her motto is "to love each other as if it's your last day, because it just could be."

Grace for the Journey

Website: www.sherrymedley.com
Email: info@sherrymedley.com

Endnotes

1. Rick Warren-Daily Hope with Rick: Best Expressions of Love is Time: October 12, 2016
2. Recorded by Danny Gokey: My Best Days-Released March 2, 2010, Written by Lari White, Chuck Cannon and Vicky McGehee-RCA/Nashville
3. Burial Planning.com: https://www.burialplanning.com/blog/15-unique-ideas-for-honoring-the-memory-of-a-loved-one
4. Quotes by Kenji Miyazawa-www.goodreads.com
5. Wired that way-The Personality Profile: Maria Littauer and Florence Littauer: May 2006-Baker Publishing Groups
6. Widowhood and Depression: New Light on Gender Differences, Selection, and Psychological Adjustment: published online June 28, 2013: https://www.ncbi.nlm.nih.gov/pmc/articles/PMC3894126/: Isaac Sasson and Debra J. Umberson
7. Karen Salmansohn-notsalmon.com
   Vicki Harrison: 21 Absolutely Heart wrenching Quotes on Loss and Grief:
8. The impact of widowhood on depression: findings from a prospective survey/https://pubmed.ncbi.nlm.nih.gov/10576303/ K B Carnelley 1, C B Wortman, R C Kessler: PMID: 10576303: NIH-National Library of Medicine: National Center for Biotechnology information
9. Merriam-Webster All-In-One Dictionary & Thesaurus: Second Edition:12/2013: Federal Street Press
10. Psychology Today-Self Care101: Maria Baratta, Ph.D. LCSW, May 27,2018: article-Skinny Revisited

www.ingramcontent.com/pod-product-compliance
Lightning Source LLC
Chambersburg PA
CBHW072013110526
44592CB00012B/1286